(Ing)

P9-DEB-465

The Procrastinator's Guide to

WILLS AND

ESTATE PLANNING

The Procrastinator's

Guide to

WILLS AND

ESTATE PLANNING

Eric G. Matlin, Attorney-at-Law

NEW AMERICAN LIBRARY

BRIDGEWATER PUBLIC LIBRARY
15 SOUTH STREET
BRIDGEWATER, MA 02324

NEW AMERICAN LIBRARY

Published by New American Library, a division of

Penguin Group (USA) Inc., 375 Hudson Street, New York, New York 10014, U.S.A.

Penguin Books Ltd, 80 Strand, London WC2R 0RL, England

Penguin Books Australia Ltd, 250 Camberwell Road,

Camberwell, Victoria 3124, Australia

Penguin Books Canada Ltd, 10 Alcorn Avenue, Toronto, Ontario, Canada M4V 3B2

Penguin Books (N.Z.) Ltd, Cnr Rosedale and Airborne Roads,

Albany, Auckland 1310, New Zealand

Penguin Books Ltd, Registered Offices: 80 Strand, London WC2R 0RL, England

First published by New American Library, a division of Penguin Group (USA) Inc.

First Printing, May 2004

10 9 8 7 6 5 4 3 2 1

Copyright © Eric G. Matlin, 2004

All rights reserved

REGISTERED TRADEMARK—MARCA REGISTRADA

LIBRARY OF CONGRESS CATALOGING-IN-PUBLICATION DATA:

Matlin, Eric.
    The procrastinator's guide to wills and estate planning/Eric Matlin.
      p. cm.
    ISBN 0-451-21059-X
    1. Estate planning—United States—Popular works. I. Title.
    KF750.Z9M48 2004
    346.7305'2—dc22   2003025669

Set in Sabon

Printed in the United States of America

Without limiting the rights under copyright reserved above, no part of this publication may be reproduced, stored in or introduced into a retrieval system, or transmitted, in any form, or by any means (electronic, mechanical, photocopying, recording, or otherwise), without the prior written permission of both the copyright owner and the above publisher of this book.

PUBLISHER'S NOTE

This publication is designed to provide accurate and authoritative information in regard to the subject matter covered. It is sold with the understanding that the publisher is not engaged in rendering legal, accounting or other professional services. If you require legal advice or other expert assistance, you should seek the services of a competent professional.

BOOKS ARE AVAILABLE AT QUANTITY DISCOUNTS WHEN USED TO PROMOTE PRODUCTS OR SERVICES. FOR INFORMATION PLEASE WRITE TO PREMIUM MARKETING DIVISION, PENGUIN GROUP (USA) INC., 375 HUDSON STREET, NEW YORK, NEW YORK 10014.

The scanning, uploading and distribution of this book via the Internet or via any other means without the permission of the publisher is illegal and punishable by law. Please purchase only authorized electronic editions, and do not participate in or encourage electronic piracy of copyright materials. Your support of the author's rights is appreciated.

AUTHOR'S NOTE

I hope you enjoy this book and that it will inspire you to do the estate planning you know must be done.

I have attempted to make this book as readable as possible, without getting bogged down in too much detail. I avoid euphemisms such as "pass on" and instead use words like "die." It makes things more real and understandable. The real-life stories described in this book are fictitious adaptations from my own experiences as an estate-planning attorney.

Some essential concepts of estate planning are relatively simple, and I've tried to be thorough and straightforward in those areas. Other complex concepts, which I don't regard as essential to the purposes of this book, are described in the leanest terms possible. An entire book can be, and in most cases has been, devoted to those subjects.

My message is not aimed at the estate-planning professional. Rather, it is written for you, one of millions of Americans who *know* they need estate planning, but never quite get around to starting or finishing it, using one excuse or another. Procrastination can—and, in this case, *must*—be overcome.

My goal is to help you overcome the procrastination that's kept you—and continues to keep you—from completing one of the most critical responsibilities you have to your family, your friends, your favorite causes and charities—and yourself.

As you will see, I am not a big believer in doing your own estate planning without the help of professionals. While I strive to learn from my mistakes in both my personal and professional life, I do occasionally make mistakes. *Do not rely exclusively* on what you read in this book. You will still have to consult an attorney, but this book will help you save time, reducing legal fees. (Just don't send me the bill!)

This book is dedicated to my loving wife, Glo. Without you, all of the wonderful things in my life would not be possible. Thank you for being my partner in the journey. I love you.

Thank you to all of the rest of my family, friends, clients, colleagues, heroes, inspirations, and passing acquaintances of all races, faiths, and cultures, those still here and those of blessed memory.

ACKNOWLEDGMENTS

Thank you to Mike Robbins, Joe Bean, Evelyn Alford, Tracy Bernstein, and attorneys Amy Kasallis, Julie Kolodziej, Lois Solomon, Audrey Young, and Michael Zelmar, for their editing assistance; to psychologist Thomas D. Yarnell, Ph.D., for his insights regarding procrastination; to anyone quoted in this book; and to my literary agent, Laura Dail, for making this possible.

CONTENTS

The Procrastinator's Guide to

WILLS AND
ESTATE PLANNING

CHAPTER 1

The (Needlessly) High Cost of Procrastination

"Procrastination is the thief of time."
—Edward Young, *Night Thoughts*

If you do not have a will, then one will be "written" for you by the laws of intestate succession in the state where you live. Below is an example of a procrastinator who died in Illinois without a valid will or funded trust.

LAST WILL AND TESTAMENT OF
PAULINE PROCRASTINATOR

As "written" for her by the legislature of the State of Illinois because she died without a valid will or funded trust

I, Pauline Procrastinator, of Anywhere Heights, Illinois, hereby do make, publish and declare this to be my Last Will and Testament.

Article 1
My Family

My spouse is Paul Procrastinator. I have two children now living, namely, Peter (age 6) and Patrick (age 4).

Article 2

Distribution of my Financial and Personal Assets

I give my husband one-half (½) of my assets which I own in my own name, and I give my children the remaining one-half (½), to be divided equally among them, regardless of any special needs that any of my children may have.

Included in my assets is a very special diamond-and-sapphire ring, which has been a family heirloom for several generations. Since I have two sons and no daughters, I had intended to give this ring to my firstborn granddaughter. Instead, since I did not do any planning, my husband may give the ring to his next wife, who in turn may give it to her daughter from a previous marriage; she can even sell it if she so chooses.

Another important asset of mine is the vacation cottage in South Haven, Michigan. I inherited that cottage from my grandparents and it has been in my family for three generations. I have very fond memories of spending time at this cottage, and I had hoped that my children and grandchildren in turn would build memories of their own on the beautiful shores of Lake Michigan. Unfortunately, since my husband is not as fond as I am of the cottage, he can sell it if he wants, depriving my children and grandchildren of this important link to their past.

When my children reach age eighteen (18), they shall have full rights to withdraw and spend all of the money that I have left to them in their shares of my estate. They may spend this money in any way that they see fit, including, but not limited to: motorcycles, sports cars, and parties for themselves and two hundred of their closest friends. No one shall have any right to question my children about how they spend their money. Also, if any of my children are disabled, then that child's share of the inheritance may result in a disqualification from government benefit programs until the share is depleted.

Should my husband remarry, and also die without a will, his second wife then shall be entitled to one-half (½) of everything my husband owns in his own name, including that amount which he inherited from me.

My husband's second wife shall not be bound to spend any part of her share on my children's behalf, even if they need the money for their health, education, or support.

The second wife shall have sole right to decide who is to get her share, even to the exclusion of my children.

Article 3
My Children

My husband, if he is still living at the time of my death, is appointed as guardian of our children. Although I love my husband and absolutely trust that he will care for our children, my husband could be required to report to the probate court each and every year following my death until our children turn eighteen (18). My husband also could be required to provide the court with an accounting of how, why, and where he spent the money necessary for the proper care of our children.

As an additional safeguard, our children shall have the right to demand and receive a complete accounting from their father of all his financial transactions regarding their share of my estate. He also may be required to post a costly surety bond each year to guarantee that he exercise proper judgment in the handling, investing, and spending of the children's money.

Should my husband die before me, or die while any of our children are minors (or die at the same time as me), I have not exercised my right to nominate who will then become the guardian of my children.

In the event that both my husband and I die before our children reach the age of eighteen (18), rather than nominating a guardian of my preference, I direct my relatives and friends, and my deceased husband's relatives and friends, to get together and select a guardian by mutual agreement, if they can all agree. Whomever they collectively nominate to raise my children will have to be fine with me.

In the event that our relatives and friends fail to agree on a guardian, I direct the judge in the probate court to make the selection. If necessary, large portions of my estate may be expended for attorney fees in this process. Finally, if the court wishes, it may appoint strangers and send my children to live in separate homes.

Article 4
Personal Representative

I decline to exercise my right to choose an executor or administrator, who is the person(s) or bank that will collect my estate, pay my bills, and distribute what is remaining to my spouse and children. Although the job of personal representative may be critical to the efficient administration of my probate estate and I know several people who would do a good job, I trust that the probate court will make that selection. Of course, the probate court may, in fact, choose a person or bank that I personally despise.

Article 5
Taxes, Costs, and Legal Fees

Under existing tax law, there are certain legitimate avenues open to me to lower federal estate taxes. Since I prefer to have my money used for governmental purposes rather than for the benefit of my husband and children, I direct that no effort be made to lower taxes.

During the entire course of the probate and guardianship proceedings, my surviving family will hire a lawyer who will handle the various court proceedings and prepare a good number of documents. I recognize that these legal fees will come straight out of my estate, and, in fact, shall be given priority and paid in full first, before any other distributions are made.

> By the State of Illinois,
> on behalf of
> Pauline Procrastinator,
> who died without a will

If you're one of those people who just can't seem to get around to planning your estate, you're not alone. Approximately 70 percent of all American adults have no estate plan—no will, no trust, no powers of attorney, nothing at all. The remaining 30 percent of the American public? My experience tells me that most of them probably have estate plans that are so incomplete or out-of-date as to be little better than no plan at all.

Large numbers of us delay everything from changing the oil in our cars to getting proper exercise. So why focus on estate planning in particular? Good question.

The answer: *If you wait too long* to plan your estate, or fail to update it periodically, your true intentions may be disregarded. You may *want* to cut taxes, you may *want* to avoid court costs and family aggravation, you may *want* to have a say in who will care for your child, you may *want* to prevent your son from spending his inheritance buying rounds of drinks at his neighborhood tavern. But if you wait too long, that's too bad, because you won't be able to do anything about it.

It's time for you to take a deep breath and say to yourself, "I could die today." Putting off *thinking* about dying is not going to put off the actual event. In fact, you will probably never be as competent as you are right now. At the very least, you will probably never be *more* competent than you are now. If your attitude is "I'll be dead, so who cares?" this book is not for you. If you care about what happens to your money or your children or your partner when you die, keep reading.

If you wait too long, the estate you spent a lifetime building could be decimated by legal fees or taxes that might have been avoided. If you become incapacitated, your family may be required to make difficult decisions about your future without taking into account your preferences. Upon your death, your family can be dragged into a time-consuming court proceeding known as probate. They'll be forced to accept the court's rulings about how your assets are to be divided, even if it means a relative you neither liked nor trusted gets a full share. Your children could end up living with the last person you would have chosen as their guardian. If you are unmarried and have no blood relatives, the state might even claim your estate, at the expense of friends or charities that could have benefited.

If you wait too long, you've fatally procrastinated. The failure to properly plan your estate is both risky and self-centered. If you tell yourself, "There's no rush, I'll take care of it soon," remember this: Estate planning is one task where the deadline often comes without warning—and there is no extension.

What's Your Excuse?

People procrastinate and delay estate planning for all sorts of reasons. Here are some of the most common excuses I've encountered, along with a snappy rebuttal.

• *"I have so little money it just isn't worthwhile for me."*
It is true that protecting a large estate from taxes is one reason for estate planning—we cover this in more detail in chapter 10—but it's certainly not the only reason or even the most important one. Your estate plan will determine how your estate, regardless of its size, will be divided, and it will speak for you when you're unable to speak for yourself.

What if your estate turns out to be much larger than you imagined? If you're killed in an accident, for example, there might be a large insurance payout or legal settlement. Or perhaps you have stock options that could increase dramatically in value. With a well-crafted estate plan in place, your estate will be prepared for virtually any contingency.

- *"I'm too young to worry about this."*

No one likes to confront dying, and so by failing to plan, you are able (temporarily) to avoid thinking about your death. Many people die before they reach their "golden years." Without an estate plan, your family's grief will be compounded by your failure to plan. If you have a family or other loved ones who depend on you, you have responsibilities, and you need to act with their welfare in mind. Adults plan their estates—it's time to be an adult!

One common type of procrastinator is the young family with little kids, a big mortgage, and bigger term insurance policies. The beneficiary of the life insurance is the spouse. The contingent beneficiaries are the children. That means that if both spouses die, leaving their young children, they also leave a big mess—a guardianship estate, generating big legal fees with an end result that the children get the remaining money at age 18 with no strings attached—party time!

- *"I don't have a family, so estate planning is not an issue."*

Estate planning isn't always about looking out for your family after you die—although that is an important part of it. Certain estate-planning tools can benefit you while you're still alive. For example, let's say you're in the hospital for an operation, and the doctor sees a potential complication that must be addressed— but you're under anesthetic. He needs your permission to proceed but you can't give it. What happens? Without the proper estate-planning documents in place, you'll need a second operation. ("Mr. Smith, the good news is that the six-hour operation was a success. The bad news is that as soon as you have recovered from the incision, we have to operate on you again.")

With the right documents, a trusted agent might be able to give consent for the second procedure. In chapter 6 we'll look into this and other ways that an estate plan can help protect you during your lifetime.

Even if you don't have any dependents, surely you have some preference about who'll get your hard-earned assets when you die: a favorite cousin, a lifelong friend, a parent, a devoted employee, or charity. Without an estate plan, you've relinquished any voice in the matter. Make no mistake, if you don't do the planning, the government often gets a larger than necessary chunk, and lawyers can be involved to a greater extent than you would wish. The courts determine both how your property is controlled and who divides it.

- *"Thinking about it just makes me too anxious. I'd rather enjoy life."*

While you might not enjoy the process, you may find that you get considerable satisfaction from the result. In fact, procrastinators looking for added motivation to get their estate planning done should consider this: You just might sleep better at night. Researchers have found that most procrastinators are not at all carefree about their inability to get things done. Unlike the fabled grasshopper who frittered away the summer without a care (only to find himself in dire straits come winter), procrastinators tend to suffer considerable anxiety about the crucial tasks they just can't seem to complete.

In fact, when a person finishes the estate planning process, he is typically relieved. It doesn't matter if it's a simple will with powers of attorney or a complex set of documents designed to save an estate hundreds of thousands of dollars or even millions of dollars—you can feel good doing it!

To summarize: Everyone has to deal with estate matters at some point (whether it's you planning ahead of time, or your heirs trying to do their best after your death), so why not do it now and not have to worry about it down the road? Once it's done, you can maximize its effectiveness by keeping it up-to-date, but that's usually not a difficult process.

In most cases, it takes a little of your time and requires a reasonable legal fee—both modest costs for the peace of mind you'll gain. Taking care of this vitally important personal business *before* any emergency arises allows you to clear your mind so that you can turn your attention toward the more enjoyable facets of life . . . like cleaning the garage or having a root canal.

A Call to Action!

If this book gathers dust on your bookshelf without being acted upon, then your good intentions in making this purchase will have failed. My goal is to help you do the appropriate amount of estate planning as your circumstances require. I have included thirteen "Action Plans" in this book, one for every chapter, which offer concrete instructions that will get you moving in the right direction, often within a defined time frame. I would suggest that as you sit down to read this book, you have Post-it notes handy to mark certain pages. Especially mark any action plans that require completion and also the page you last read, so you can easily pick up where you left off. If you intend to read this book in one sitting, you are probably setting yourself up to fail. Take your time, but keep moving through the steps suggested.

A reasonable time horizon for finishing your estate plan from the time you begin this book is about one to three months (in other words, at least one action plan a week). The longer you go past that time frame, the less likely it is that you will ever finish.

Action Plan One: Let's Get Started!

This is an easy one and should be done immediately!

1. Grab a pen or pencil and some notepaper. For me, a legal pad works well. Use whatever works best for you. Think about some of the reasons that—even before reading this book—you already know you need an estate plan. Jot them down.

2. Pull out your calendar and mark a preliminary deadline for completing your estate plan. Over the next week, tell others about the deadline you have set for yourself in doing your estate plan.

CHAPTER 2

Understanding Procrastination and Overcoming It

"To know what needs to be done, and then to do it, comprises the whole philosophy of practical life."
—William Osler

Procrastination is the chronic postponement of necessary tasks—generally those considered difficult or unpleasant. We waste so much time trying to avoid these tasks that our failure in doing them is assured.

Just about all of us put off an unpleasant task at some point in our lives. Occasional and short-term delays aren't necessarily disastrous. The real trouble comes when repeated procrastination begins to have a negative effect on your life.

According to one recent academic study, approximately 40 percent of the population cause themselves some sort of loss through procrastination, and more than 25 percent experience chronic and debilitating procrastination.

Such statistics help illustrate just why procrastination has been called the nation's single most common time-management problem. For those with a serious problem, procrastination

causes considerable anxiety, leading to reduced personal pro-
ductivity. The anxiety itself becomes the biggest roadblock to
completing the task.

The Top Twelve

Below is my top-twelve list of the most common reasons that
people delay estate planning. What is your reaction to each of
these reasons? Do any sound familiar to you?

12. Most people don't like to think about death or money. Wills
and trusts force you to confront mortality and money, two issues
that can be difficult to face. This is particularly true if you are
healthy and don't feel you have much money.

**11. Estate planning is something most people are unfamiliar with
or feel uncomfortable about.** Because you don't know much about
estate-planning documents, you may experience anxiety or struggle with feelings of inadequacy when confronted with the subject.
You know how to be a good plumber or schoolteacher or police
officer or how to run a restaurant, but you don't know estate
planning.

10. There's no hard-and-fast deadline. Many people can't accomplish anything until a deadline looms. But when it comes to wills
and trusts, the crucial and final deadline often comes without
warning.

9. It's not much fun. True, but life isn't always fun, especially if you
are an adult. If you need fun, plan a party to celebrate finishing
your estate plan.

8. People hate lawyers. But not *all* people hate *all* lawyers; you *can*
find one you can relate to.

7. People are afraid of massive amounts of paper. If you understand the paperwork, it becomes less intimidating. Be prepared to ask questions about anything you don't understand.

6. You won't live to see the largest benefits of your estate plan. The main beneficiaries will be your heirs. It can be difficult to devote yourself to this task until you accept your family's priorities as your own.

5. It might mean making decisions that could arouse negative feelings in loved ones. Maybe you're concerned your family will be angry when they learn the details of your estate plan.

4. The size of the job can be daunting. Estate planning can be, but isn't necessarily, a big, time-consuming task. The perceived enormity of the task can prevent some people from even starting the job.

3. Not doing your estate planning can be a form of passive-aggressive behavior. If you're not happy with your future heirs, failing to complete necessary wills or trusts can be a subconscious way to punish them.

2. Some people just like to live for the moment. Some procrastinators simply can't—or won't—force themselves to pass up short-term pleasure and sit down to complete their estate planning, even if at some level they understand that doing so will provide them with far greater long-term satisfaction.

1. Guilt feeds upon itself. The real number one excuse for not doing an estate plan, when you know you need one, is the wall built from guilt about not doing estate planning, adding to any depression you might have about procrastination in other areas of your life and leading, ironically, to further delay. If you can't move from that state, a psychologist or counselor with experience working with procrastinators might help you.

All of these reasons to delay are perfectly understandable—but that doesn't make them any less dangerous or counterproductive. Fortunately, it is possible to use your natural fears to your benefit.

You know that doing nothing can make your worst fears come true. But whatever you fear about estate planning, the danger from your own inaction will always be greater. Just weigh the very real dangers of delay against the fear of thinking about money or mortality, and you might discover that doing your estate plan is easier not only in the long term, which is obvious, but also in the short term, since the whole subject can then be put behind you.

Why We Procrastinate

We waste so much time trying to avoid difficult and unpleasant tasks that we set ourselves up for failure. Clinical psychologist Thomas D. Yarnell, Ph.D., has studied the subject of procrastination extensively. According to Dr. Yarnell, there are two major causes of procrastination:

- *Avoidance:* We procrastinate to avoid overwhelming, difficult, or unpleasant tasks and to avoid change.
- *Fear and anxiety:* We procrastinate because of our fear of failure, fear of success, fear of criticism, fear of making mistakes, and fear of rejection.

Let's cut to the chase. Here is a short list of techniques inspired by Dr. Yarnell that you can follow now to end procrastination and start this ball rolling. Since we are not all the same, Dr. Yarnell's advice is to keep the suggestions that work for you and forget the rest. The techniques will help you as you complete the action plans in this book, and when you have finished your estate plan, these tips will help you finish other tasks that have been delayed by procrastination.

1. Do the easiest part first so you can get started. Once you are moving, it's easier to continue.
2. Next, take the tasks you find most unpleasant or difficult and break them down into small steps to then be tackled one at a time.
3. Give yourself a deadline and let others know it.
4. Get help. There is no rule that you must do everything yourself. For example, much of the information-gathering needed in chapter 3 could be delegated to other people, such as your banker, broker, insurance agent, and so on. Make a very specific list of those you can call upon.
5. Get organized so you can take advantage of momentum. There is nothing worse for a procrastinator than to get started, only to discover that you don't have everything you need to complete the task. You then have to stop, get the needed materials or information, and start again. Get organized, get started, and keep going until you finish.
6. Use this book! I have broken up the task of estate planning into component pieces. If you take this book chapter by chapter, you'll find that no single task is overwhelming.

HOW TO DEFEAT PROCRASTINATION

Do unpleasant tasks first and get them over with.

Overcoming Estate-Planning Procrastination

While there are do-it-yourself will and trust form books and software packages, they can be confusing for the average person and a poor option for anyone who varies from what the author or designer believes to be a "normal" or "average" person. Moreover, it can be a waste of time or worse to attempt the admittedly complex task of estate planning without the assistance of an expert.

There might be little things an estate-planning lawyer will notice that are missing from a form document. For example, most estate-planning attorneys use an attestation clause (affidavit) at the end of a will that allows the will to be validated without the necessity of bringing the witnesses to testify that they saw you sign the document. Without such a clause, the witnesses may have to testify. Some form books, even some marketed to lawyers, leave out this simple affidavit or put it in a separate section, where it might be overlooked.

Estate planning can be a complicated process, but if the complexities of the process are holding up your estate plan, there is a simple, two-step solution to your problem:

First, use this book to help you sort through the issues of estate planning, get organized, and understand your options. If you walk into a meeting with an estate-planning attorney without having done any information-gathering and background work on your own, your estate plan may not be as good as it could have been if you had initially invested the time to understand the concepts involved and to get organized.

Second, hire an estate-planning attorney. The right attorney can help you get motivated and move forward. Estate-planning attorneys have dealt with many or all of the issues that are likely to confront you. They not only understand the laws, but also know how to make the laws work best for you. They have dealt with different family situations and dynamics and have assisted their clients in overcoming procrastination.

REAL-LIFE STORIES

Zack and Arielle are in their forties and have children aged 16, 13, and 4. Their form of estate-planning procrastination is extremely common: While they had relatively little trouble determin-

REAL-LIFE STORIES

ing who would handle their assets, they could not decide on a guardian for the kids. Their attorney was able to convince them that even an imperfect decision was better than no decision at all.

How? By pointing out to them that if they failed to make a choice, not only would the decision be out of their hands, it would be totally out of their children's hands as well.

The two older children were old enough that the clients wanted them to have a say in the guardianship decision. At the time of the will, however, there were too many unresolved factors for Zack and Arielle to impose a binding decision. Thus, the final document included language to the effect that any guardianship decision should be made in consultation with the children. They also discussed the fact that without proper planning, their children might not only be left without their parents, but also without their siblings. So the document noted that Zack and Arielle strongly desired that their children not be separated. The prospect of leaving their children without each other in homes they didn't like was enough to spur the couple to action.

If you're someone who avoids attorneys and attorneys' fees whenever possible, consider that hiring an estate-planning attorney isn't like hiring most other lawyers. Usually an attorney is hired when it's necessary to go to court. Estate-planning attorneys are hired, at least in part, to keep your family *out* of court. And while any dealing with an attorney is likely to cost you money, the odds are good that an estate-planning attorney will, in the end, save you more in taxes and probate costs than she charged as a fee—possibly much more.

Don't let a dislike of lawyers cause you to delay your estate planning. Find an estate-planning attorney. In the next chapter, we'll discuss the best way for a procrastinator to hire the right lawyer.

Action Plan Two: Ask Yourself Some Tough Questions

1. Write down some of the reasons that you have procrastinated in doing your estate plan.

2. Envision the mess that could be created if you died today. If you are able to, write down a few of the worst scenarios that you can imagine if this were to happen.

3. Preliminarily, answer the question, "Is this something I can do on my own, or should I hire an attorney?" If you think you have already decided to do estate planning on your own, put another entry into your calendar for six weeks from now. If you have not made substantial progress by then, speak to a lawyer within two weeks after that. Put that deadline into your calendar as well.

4. List, in order of importance, all the things that matter most to you in the world. Most people with families put their spouse and children near the top of such a list. If that's true of your list, ask yourself: Do your actions square with your stated values? If your family means that much to you, shouldn't you put aside your own idiosyncrasies for a while and get your estate planning done?

5. If you can't resolve any difficult or sensitive family issues that seem to hinder your progress, put them aside for now. Look at it this way: No matter what decisions you eventually come to regarding your family, you're better off doing estate planning than not doing it. Yes, it can be difficult to decide whether or not to disinherit a child or precisely how to divvy up your estate, but dying without a will only ensures that your voice will never be heard on the subject. Whatever your decision, it's always better that you decide *something*. If you change your mind later, you can change your documents.

CHAPTER 3

Getting Started

"The beginning is the most important part of the work."
—Plato, *The Republic*

Getting started with the process of estate planning involves organizing your records and finding a way to complete the job. In this chapter, I'll help you get organized. In later chapters, I'll help you continue a path toward finishing the job.

I'll help you bring together all the information you're going to need to complete the plan—information about you, your family, your finances.

I'll suggest a framework for getting the job done. For some, that might mean using a workbook or a computer program designed for do-it-yourself estate planning, but for most people it will mean selecting an attorney.

Nothing you'll need to do in this chapter requires any detailed knowledge of estate-planning tools or techniques, so there's no reason to put off these tasks. I'll break the process into small, manageable tasks, and offer step-by-step guidance to avoid any confusion about how to proceed.

Let's Get Organized

There are at least three good reasons to get all your personal and financial data together.

First, you can better determine what estate-planning tools are appropriate if you organize your personal finances. We'll take a look at various estate-planning tools in later chapters.

Second, assuming you choose to hire an attorney to help you with your estate plan, the information you compile will make the task easier on both you and the lawyer. If you are prepared before walking in the door, you will get off to a better start— and possibly a lower attorney's bill as well.

Third, if something were to happen to you, this list could serve as a reference for your family in handling your affairs, even if it has no legal weight. One thing worse than leaving no estate plan is leaving no clue to the whereabouts of your assets. That's a nightmare.

HOW TO DEFEAT PROCRASTINATION

Get organized so you can take advantage of momentum. Nothing is worse for a procrastinator than to get started—at last— and discover you don't have everything you need to finish. You have to stop, find what you need, and then try to start again . . . days, weeks, or even years later. So get organized. Keep the momentum going until you finish.

The following questions should help you bring together most, if not all, information relevant to your estate plan. Some things you can answer without reference materials, but you'll need to do a little research to obtain all the information.

I've divided the work into three sections: personal data, financial data, and fiduciary data. Do one section at a time.

Have everything you need for the project within arm's reach

when you begin. This means fewer delays to search down missing pieces once you're under way, and it lowers the risk of becoming distracted by other tasks when you're away from your desk.

For this part of the task, you'll need a calculator. Also, grab your personal phone book so you have names, addresses, and telephone numbers of family and friends at your fingertips. Get any old wills or trusts or powers of attorney, if you have done these types of documents in the past. And assemble account statements and other records relating to your possessions.

I encourage you (in a rare exception to copyright law!) to copy these pages and bring them with you when you meet with the attorney. If you prefer, write the answers on a separate piece of paper—don't feel constrained by the boxes.

Questionnaire One—Personal and Family Data

You'll need this important information about yourself:

Information needed	Your information
List your full name, date of birth, and social security number in addition to any previous or other names by which you are, or have been, known. List alternate names and social security numbers, if applicable. This can help ensure that all of your assets are accounted for after your death.	
If you're married, list your spouse's name and any prior names for him or her as well. Also list his or her social security numbers.	
List your addresses and telephone numbers for both home and work, plus any other residences in or out of state. Include cell phone numbers and e-mail addresses, if appropriate.	
If you or your spouse is not a U.S. citizen, make a note of that, too.	

Information needed *(continued)*	Your information *(continued)*
If applicable, list previous spouses' names, as well as when you were divorced or when the previous spouse died.	

It's always in your interest to make it as simple as possible for your attorney to contact you. This ensures she'll be able to get answers to questions quickly, keeping billable hours, if any, as low as possible. If you work or have addresses in other states, it could impact your estate planning.

Be prepared to provide details concerning any previous marriages involving either you or your spouse. Include the basics of any divorce settlements; it's possible they could affect your estate plan. For example, your divorce settlement might require that you take out a life-insurance policy naming any child by that marriage as beneficiary. Failure to consider divorce settlements when doing estate planning could result in your estate plan being contested or even invalidated. Be prepared to discuss with the lawyer some details of any of the breakups that were particularly adversarial.

If you have children, you'll need to provide this information:

List full names of each child	
Date of birth of each child	
Social security number of each child	
Current address of each child	
Telephone numbers of each child	
Any special needs, such as a physical or mental handicap, for each child	

This is a good time to start thinking about how you would like to treat your children in your will. Will they all be treated the same? Does one have a special need that merits a different amount, or different assets under different conditions?

Would you like to exclude any or all of your children from your estate? Be prepared to provide some details here. An estate-planning attorney can discuss specific options with you on this front, but it's best to have thought through your intentions in advance—disinheriting a child or other close family member shouldn't be a spur-of-the-moment decision.

Occasionally, parents who wish to disinherit a child will simply ignore the child in the plan. This could be a mistake. Laws vary from state to state, but it's often necessary to explicitly state in your wills or trusts your intention not to include a child. You can leave a child nothing, but if you simply treat the child as if he doesn't exist, this child won't necessarily be cut out of your estate. He might be able to argue that you just forgot about him.

Do either you or your spouse have children outside this marriage?

List full names	
Dates of birth	
Names of parents	
Social security numbers	
Current addresses	
Telephone numbers	
Any special needs, such as a physical or mental handicap	

To what degree would you like to include or exclude these children from your estate? Would you like them to be treated the same as your children from your current marriage? Differently? Even if these children have never been part of your life—or your current family doesn't know about them—they should at least be mentioned. Otherwise, your family could find out about them the hard way, when they challenge your will after you're gone.

If you have any deceased children, make a note of it. It is particularly important to the estate-planning process if that child had descendants.

Do you have grandchildren or great-grandchildren?

List full names	
Dates of birth	
Names of parents	
Social security numbers	
Current addresses	
Telephone numbers	
Any special needs, such as a physical or mental handicap	

Do you want to make bequests to any grandchildren or great-grandchildren independent of the bequests being made to your children? Are any grandchildren or great-grandchildren being treated differently from the others—or do you intend to cut any out of your estate? If so, provide the details here.

Would you prefer to divide your assets evenly between your

children's families, or so that every grandchild gets the same amount? For example, if you have two children, one with one child and one with four, is your estate still divided in two, with a 50 percent share going to each child together with his family?

If your estate is large enough that some of it will likely filter down to the next generation, that's important. Most people look to their children's generation, but some look farther into the future in making this decision. Only you can decide what is most fair.

Do you have parents, siblings, stepchildren, nieces and nephews, other relatives, or close friends you wish to have included in your estate plan?

List full names and relationship	
Dates of birth	
Names of parents	
Social security numbers	
Current addresses	
Telephone numbers	
Any special needs, such as a physical or mental handicap	

If you wish anyone other than a spouse or child to inherit some portion of your estate, you must have an estate plan—if you die without an estate plan, these intended beneficiaries will often be cut out entirely, depending on which state you live in.

Is there any person you wish to exclude from your estate plan who otherwise might expect to be included? Is there any person who you fear may try to thwart your wishes? Is there anyone you feel may try to influence your personal finances a little more than you would prefer? Jot down brief details, but be prepared to talk about the situation more extensively with your attorney.

It is a good idea to explain in your will or trust why you're choosing to exclude an individual, but be careful to avoid anything that could be considered libelous. If strife can be expected, there are steps that can be taken to reduce these troublemakers' chances of success. This can be a difficult topic to consider, since no one likes to think about the relatives we don't get along with, or those who simply can't be trusted. But it's far better to confront such matters now than it is to leave your heirs in a battle royal after you're gone.

Are any of your beneficiaries in a position where you prefer they not take direct control of the assets you intend to leave them? In the case of minors, you will typically want to postpone their inheritance. It is up to you to decide at what ages your beneficiaries should receive their shares of your estate. You also can restrict control of assets for adults. If you would like to explore this possibility, explain briefly why you think it might be a good idea to restrict control of assets left to these people—for example, have they always been irresponsible with money? Do they have a history of substance abuse?

List full names	
Dates of birth	
Names of parents	
Restrict to a certain age because:	
Restrict with other conditions such as:	

Also give some idea how much control you wish these people to have—should they have free access over some portion of the assets, but not all? Should they have no access except for certain purposes? Do they need someone watching over every withdrawal?

There's no need to be precise here; just jot down some ideas. Failure to plan ahead in this area means that every adult inheriting from you will receive his share without limitations soon after your death.

Warning: Dying without proper estate-planning documents in place likely means that each of your children will receive the same amount from your estate, even if one of them has spent his life in faithful service to the family business, and another hasn't called for the past twenty years.

The law does not attempt to determine what each child deserves. If you haven't bothered to provide guidance through an estate plan, your spouse and children will inherit according to the preset formula under your state law.

Also note that if you have a spouse or children, no one else is likely to get a thing unless you spell it out. See State Survey #1 following the glossary.

Do you wish to include any charitable organizations as beneficiaries?

List full names	
Current addresses	
Telephone numbers	
Any special requests or limitations as to how the money is used?	

If you know what you want to leave to them and the specific purpose of the gift, indicate this also—your lawyer might suggest specific strategies for leaving assets to charity that will optimize the gift from everyone's perspective.

Congratulations! You've finished this section. Take a break. Reward yourself, as you promised yourself. And feel better knowing you are one step closer to completing your estate plan.

Questionnaire Two—Assets, Liabilities, and Other Financial Data

You probably know the approximate value of your estate. But with estate planning, details are essential. Of particular interest: If you're married, you'll have to specify the ownership details of each asset mentioned on the list. That means spelling out whether an item is owned by you, either individually or through a trust; owned by your spouse—again, individually or through a trust; or owned jointly by the two of you together.

An asset's value is not what you paid for it, but what it is worth *today* on the open market (the asset's "fair market value"). If determining the fair market value of an item such as an antique or a vehicle will be difficult, see if you can find something to compare it with in the newspaper classifieds or an antiques guide. If there is no ready market, you might need to obtain a professional appraisal to establish fair market value.

For most items of tangible personal property, the fair market value is likely to be less than the amount you paid. But certain assets, such as stocks, real estate, and art, can appreciate in value, sometimes dramatically.

Ascertaining the fair market value of your possessions doesn't need to be a complicated process; you are trying to determine a ballpark estimate, because your net worth will no doubt be different when you die. In most cases there is no need to have your assets professionally appraised at this point. In addition, you don't need to be concerned with relatively minor personal possessions.

Start with those items you know or believe to have a fair market value of $1,000 or more.

Do you own real estate? Provide the following information for each property that you own or any property in which you hold a partial interest.

Primary residence:	
Address	
Approximate value Is there an outstanding mortgage or other lien?	
How is title held to your residence?	
Other real estate holdings:	
Address	
Approximate value Is there a mortgage on the property?	
How is title to this property held?	

Your property-tax assessment might be a useful guide to the value of a piece of property, unless assessments have not kept up with rising real estate prices in your region. Or just ask a real estate agent, who will usually be more than willing to give you an unofficial appraisal, either because she is nice or because she hopes to get your listing someday.

If you fail to do the proper planning, particularly if you own any out-of-state property, your heirs will be required to go through additional legal hassles.

Do you have life insurance?

What type of insurance (whole life, universal, variable, or term)?	
If you have term insurance, how many years of level premiums remain?	
Do you have an irrevocable life-insurance trust (ILIT)? (see chapter 11)	
Who is the owner and beneficiary of each policy?	
Who is the contingent beneficiary of each policy?	
What is the cash value of each policy?	
What is the death benefit of each policy?	
If you're a veteran, do you have GI life insurance? What is the policy number?	

Make a list of any accidental death benefits arising from such sources as motor clubs, group health insurance policies, and credit card companies. These should not be included in the accounting of your net worth, but it is worthwhile to list them here, since they might be payable to a beneficiary and you don't want them to fall through the cracks and be overlooked by your family.

What is the source of the accidental death benefit?	
What are the appropriate membership, policy, or credit card numbers?	

What other financial assets do you own, and what are their current values?

Asset	Financial institution, account numbers, interest rates, maturities, approximate value
Money market accounts	
Savings and checking accounts	
Certificates of deposit	
Credit union accounts	
U.S. savings bonds	
Treasury bonds, notes, and bills	
Municipal and corporate bonds	
GNMAs and other U.S. agency–issued notes receivable	
Mortgages owned (this doesn't mean mortgages you owe, but those owed to you)	
Mutual fund holdings	
Stocks, as well as any other brokerage accounts not included elsewhere on the list	
Annuities	
Limited partnerships	
Business interests—note the form of the business, such as S corporation, limited liability company, partnership, or sole proprietorship.	

Asset *(continued)*	Financial institution, account numbers, interest rates, maturities, approximate value *(continued)*
IRAs—regular, rollovers, and Roths List beneficiary and contingent beneficiary, if any	
401(k)s, 403(B)s, 457 Plans, SEPs, and other "qualified" retirement plans. List the beneficiary and contingent beneficiary of each plan, if any	

It's a good idea to keep track of your cost basis, which is the amount you originally paid for the asset. When you sell the asset, the cost basis may be necessary to determine your gain or loss on the sale of the asset, which is reported on your annual income-tax return.

These details won't necessarily have much effect on your estate plan, but it's good to have the information handy for your family in case someday they need to take over your affairs. An up-to-the-minute valuation of each account isn't required. Just get the ballpark figure from a recent account statement for each, and be sure you haven't omitted any accounts. This information may also be important if you make a gift of any of these assets during your lifetime.

Do you own "special" personal property such as collections, antiques, art, or jewelry? If you have a particular beneficiary in mind for any particular piece of personal property, indicate that too. For example, perhaps there's a musically gifted grandchild who would appreciate your piano.

Description	Value/Comments	Location	Beneficiary

Don't forget to include any item of value located where your heirs might not think to look because it is either hidden for safety or not kept in your house. If you have a bank safe-deposit box, provide the details, and make sure one of your heirs will have access to it upon your death or disability (see chapter 7). You also may wish to note items with special sentimental value if you know whom you want to have them.

Do you own titled personal property, such as cars, boats, and airplanes?

Description	Value/Comments	Location	Beneficiary

With respect to other personal possessions, such as consumer electronics, appliances, furniture, and clothing, there's no need for a complete listing. For purposes of estate planning, the values assigned to such items is roughly akin to what you might pay for them at a garage sale, so don't let yourself get bogged down trying to decide a fair market value for an eight-year-old toaster oven. Assign the personal property a nominal value as a group, which for most people is usually not more than a few thousand dollars.

You should also make note of prepaid cemetery plots or funeral expenses, or season tickets to sporting events that may be valuable. Prepaid funeral arrangements should be noted, because

your heirs might need to be reminded that this has been provided for.

Now total your assets from this first part of Questionnaire
Two and enter the number here: $_____.

Are you the plaintiff or defendant in any ongoing lawsuits? If
there is a good chance that these could result in additional assets
being added to your estate, or a judgment against you reducing
your estate, your estate plan should take this into consideration.

Description	Comments	Attorney or Legal Firm

Do you anticipate inheriting money or other assets? Obviously if you have not yet received an expected inheritance, the
projected receipt of the inheritance should be noted but not fig-
ured into your assets or net worth.

Description	Amount	Source

Of course, you may not know all of the details in advance,
but provide as accurate an estimate as possible.

Do you know how the inheritance will be transferred to you?
Is there a trust, or will the property pass directly via a joint tenancy or beneficiary designation? It can be difficult to discuss details of inheritances with your parents or with anyone who
might have you in his will, but there can be sizable benefits to
doing so. For example, if you have a high net worth, you may

want to coordinate your estate plan with that of your parents and even with those of your children, if they have a high net worth, to limit estate taxes, and for other reasons.

REAL-LIFE STORIES

John Williams carefully detailed his entire estate for his attorney. They set up what seemed like an appropriate estate plan for him. But what John had failed to mention was that he was due to receive a multimillion-dollar inheritance once his parents died. Perhaps he thought it was in poor taste to discuss such things. Perhaps he was unaware of his parents' wealth. Even so, he should have found the time to update his plan as soon as his inheritance was known.

Whatever the reason, the results were unfortunate. When he died, the estate plan that had been appropriate for his previously small estate was severely lacking for a larger estate. As a result, his children paid more in estate taxes than they would have had to pay with minimal planning, eating away at a gift John's parents would have wanted to go to John's children with minimal drain.

Remember: Whenever there is a major change in your financial situation, marital status, state of residence, or intended beneficiaries, your estate plan must be reexamined.

What are your liabilities?

Description of Liability	Dollar Amount
Mortgages	

Description of Liability *(continued)*	Dollar Amount *(continued)*
Second mortgages	
Home equity loans	
Student loans	
Automobile loans	
Credit card balances	
Other notes payable	
Margin balance in brokerage accounts	
Judgments	
Other liabilities, in excess of $1,000	

Total Liabilities: $_____.

What is your estimated net worth (assets minus liabilities)? $_____

Don't worry about counting every last dollar, as your net worth is going to change between now and the time you die. Calculate your estimated net worth, and don't leave out any major financial assets or liabilities.

Do not include in your net worth any accounts for which you are custodian for a minor, such as Uniform Gifts to Minors Act (UGMA) or Uniform Transfer to Minors Act (UTMA) accounts, unless you have named yourself as custodian (which, as we will discuss in chapter 5, is not a good idea, as it may subject the account to probate upon your death). Also, do not include any account for which you act as trustee if you were not the grantor and you do not have a general power of appointment over the account (see glossary for explanation of these terms, or ask your attorney for details).

Have you filed any gift-tax returns during your lifetime? Has your spouse?

Generally, you should have filed a gift-tax return if you ever made a gift of more than $10,000 (prior to 2002; $11,000 in 2003) to any person other than your spouse in any single year. A copy of any gift-tax returns filed may be useful information to the attorney when you meet her.

Congratulations! You've finished another section. Take a break. Reward yourself, as you promised yourself. And feel better knowing you are another step closer to completing your estate plan.

Questionnaire Three—Fiduciary Data

Who are your fiduciaries? They are those persons or companies who will act on your behalf when you are unable to do so.

List a primary fiduciary and as many contingent (secondary and so on) fiduciaries as you need to feel comfortable with the roles these people will play on your behalf.

Role	Name, address, and telephone number
Guardian of your minor or disabled children	
Agent for health care to make medical decisions for you if you are unable	

Role *(continued)*	Name, address, and telephone number *(continued)*
Agent for property, who can manage your assets when you cannot and sign your name to financial transactions when you're incapacitated	
Executor for your will	
Trustee for your trust(s)	

If you haven't selected these people, jot down the names of those who seem like they might be appropriate. We'll talk about how to select fiduciaries in chapters 5, 7, and 8.

Do you have a CPA or financial planner who advises you?

Adviser	Company name, address, and telephone number	Function

If you hire an attorney to draft your estate plans, she may need to work together with your other financial professionals.

Where do you keep your important documents, such as insurance policies or previous estate plans?

Document	Location	Name, address and telephone number of person with access

We'll discuss the proper place to store such documents in chapter 14. For now, it's important that someone else knows where the documents are stored and has access to them in an emergency.

Is there anything else you consider important to your estate-planning needs? Do you have any other concerns that should be addressed?

DID YOU HAVE TROUBLE GETTING THROUGH THIS LIST?

In a perfect world, every client would walk into a lawyer's office with all the necessary information ready to go. But if gathering this information is causing you to procrastinate about your estate plan, there are only two or three things that are essential to have with you when you finally show up:

1. Your address book, so you can provide names and addresses of beneficiaries who will receive your assets and of fiduciaries who will act on your behalf if you die or become incapacitated.

2. A rough idea of your financial situation, including an estimate (say within a few thousand dollars) of the value of your estate, the size of your IRA or other retirement plan assets, and the death benefits of any life-insurance policies you own.

3. If you can easily obtain them, any prior and perhaps now out-of-date wills or other estate-plan documents.

Action Plan Three: Congratulations, You're Making Real Progress!

You deserve a treat!

1. If you have done (or delegated) most of the work in this chapter, you should feel good about your progress.
2. Reward yourself! Take a hot bath; pour yourself a cocktail; pick up the novel that you put aside to read this book; get out in the sun and smell the flowers, or plant yourself a garden if you have no flowers; veg out in front of the television; take a nap—whatever works for you!

CHAPTER 4

Getting Help . . . or Doing It Yourself?

"A man who dies without a will has lawyers for his heirs."
—Anonymous

Now that you've completed your lists, you have a decision to make: Do you get professional help by hiring an attorney—or buy a book or computer software to help you draft the documents yourself?

No law says you must use an attorney to create an estate plan. Doing it yourself *is* cheaper—probably less than $50 compared to $1,000 or more.

But be forewarned: You might just get what you pay for. Although many of the books and programs are detailed, your unique situation may be different from the models presented. And who will answer your questions? Who will catch your mistakes? A single oversight or error could cost you or your heirs more—much more—than a lawyer would have charged for a proper estate plan.

A COMPROMISE

If you want to save some money but still assure yourself of a quality estate plan, here's a "compromise" option: Do your own estate plan with one of the computer programs or other kits on the market, then pay an estate-planning attorney on an hourly basis to review your work.

Some people, generally those willing to invest considerable time in understanding some of the intricacies of estate planning, manage to do a decent job with a do-it-yourself kit. For them, a lawyer might need a few hours to review their homemade plan and possibly recommend minor changes. Of course, it can take much longer if the do-it-yourself plan was not properly prepared.

It's my experience that the do-it-yourself approach often is a poor idea for procrastinators. Before you ante up for the book or software, ask yourself if you're *really* likely to use the program once you have it. Have you purchased similar do-it-yourself kits in the past? Did you use them? Do-it-yourself income-tax reporting programs, similar in some ways to estate-planning kits, come with federally imposed deadlines that can motivate the procrastinator. Estate planning has few deadlines that arrive without irreparable repercussions.

A lot of procrastinators get stuck at this critical point because many people have little, no, or only negative experiences with lawyers and know even less about where and how to find an estate-planning lawyer.

HOW TO DEFEAT PROCRASTINATION: DON'T GET STUCK!

Keep moving ahead by finishing this chapter before you do anything else. Break unpleasant or difficult tasks into small steps and tackle them one at a time.

There's nothing wrong with a little caution: Selecting the right lawyer is a crucial part of this process, and because you'll be sharing some very personal details with the lawyer, you'll certainly want to find someone you can relate to and trust.

Don't let caution turn into stagnancy. Follow the strategies outlined in this section, and you should be able to find a lawyer suited to you and to the estate-planning task you've started.

Burger's Blunder

Just how tricky is estate planning for the nonspecialist? Even U.S. Supreme Court Chief Justice Warren Burger, certainly a prominent jurist but not an estate-planning specialist, made a number of crucial errors when he wrote his own will prior to his death in 1995.

LAST WILL AND TESTAMENT
OF
WARREN E. BURGER

I hereby make and declare the following to be my last will and testament.

1. My exeuctors will first pay all claims against my estate;

2. The remainder of my estate will be distributed as follows: one-third to my daughter, Margaret Elizabeth Burger Rose and two-thirds to my son, Wade A. Burger;

3. I designate and appoint as executors of this will, Wade A. Burger and J. Michael Luttig.

IN WITNESS WHEREOF, I have hereunto set my hand to this my Last Will and Testament this _____9th_____ day of June, 1994.

Warren E Burger
WARREN E. BURGER

We hereby certify that in our presence on the date written above WARREN E. BURGER signed the foregoing instrument and declared it to be his Last Will and Testament and that at this request in his presence and in the presence of each other we have signed our names below as witnesses.

[signature] residing at 120 'F' St, NW
Washington, DC

[signature] residing at 3041. Meetig. St
~~FAIRFAX VA~~ Falls Church, VA

SWORN TO AND SUBSCRIBED BEFORE ME THIS 9th
DAY OF June 19 94   *Constance Y. Ferguson*
NOTARY PUBLIC

CONSTANCE Y. FERGUSON
Notary Public, District of Columbia
My Commission Expires January 31, 1999

Justice Burger's will:

- failed to grant the executors powers to act independently of the court's supervision, so his heirs were forced to have the probate court approve every step of his estate's liquidation and distribution
- failed to waive bond or surety, which added insurance costs
- was not "self-proving"—that is, it didn't include a notarized affidavit by the witnesses that they signed in each other's presence—an oversight that most likely led to added court appearances and lawyers' fees and can also lead to the necessity of tracking down the witnesses to sign new affidavits or appear in court
- failed to take advantage of various techniques for reducing estate taxes, and
- left his entire estate open to public scrutiny. Anyone can contact the Arlington County, Virginia, probate court to obtain Justice Burger's complete probate file, including an inventory of his assets. Most families would prefer to keep these types of matters private.

Probate caused a drain of at least $250,000 to $300,000 on Justice Burger's estate. When all the taxes and legal costs were added up, they accounted for nearly half of his roughly $2 million estate—and the probate took over three years. If Justice Burger had made the right moves he could have saved hundreds of thousands of dollars and protected his privacy.

The Specialist

Justice Burger's story makes an obvious point: not every lawyer handles estate planning. Some states certify a legal specialty in estate planning. Certification ensures that the lawyer is taking regular classes on the subject. Since the laws governing estates change and evolve, taking classes can keep a lawyer fresh and up-to-date. However, many states do not certify an estate-planning specialty.

The Superspecialist

Even among specialists, there are superspecialists. Some estate-planning lawyers concentrate on the very latest cutting-edge tax techniques and charge accordingly. In general, they're most appropriate for those with estates worth well into the millions of dollars, and if you are in that situation, they will probably be worth every penny you spend on their services. If that's your situation, insist that your lawyer call in the big guns, at least as cocounsel.

What Will My Estate-Planning Lawyer Do?

Estate-planning lawyers are not reinventing the wheel with completely new documents for every client. Estate-planning forms and reference materials for lawyers to use are written often by the trust divisions of large, well-known banks or a particular state's continuing legal education forum.

A qualified estate-planning lawyer must do more than just fill in the blanks on these documents, however; your lawyer should:

- comprehend what each provision means and what its effects will be for you
- keep abreast of major developments in estate planning, and
- understand your family, finances, and goals to the extent necessary to draft competent legal documents and to explain the documents to your satisfaction

Finding the Lawyer Who's Right For You

Here are five steps to take. It's possible you won't need all of them. Finding the right lawyer is as important as getting all of your family and financial information together, which you've already done. The information is ready to be put to work for you, once you have a lawyer that's right for you.

1. Set a deadline for finding a lawyer. The process might take you a day or two, but it could take longer, so the best idea might be to set a target date as your deadline for having met with the attorneys to whom you were referred. Set a second deadline for making your decision. Once that's done, make an appointment and remember to write it in your calendar.

2. Restrict yourself to estate-planning specialists. It will dramatically reduce the number of lawyers from whom you have to choose. You can go outside your immediate area to find a lawyer if you're willing to make the trip, but if you live near a state border, don't cross it. A lawyer practicing in one state might not be up on all the rules in another.

3. Start networking:
   • Ask your friends who they used to do their estate planning, and if they were pleased with the results. Stick to friends in roughly the same economic situation as yourself, and, of course, ask only those whose judgment you trust.
   • If your friends can't provide any recommendations, or if you've just moved and don't yet have any close friends in the region, ask your financial professionals. If you have an accountant, financial planner, or general-practice attorney, ask any or all of them if they can provide leads.

- Another promising resource is your bank. Ask to speak to the head of the trust department or the bank manager.
- If you still can't get a referral, call your state's bar association and ask for names. A list of state bar association phone numbers is available at www.abanet.org/legalservices/public.html, the American Bar Association's Web site. Bar associations provide referrals as a free service.
- Two more suggestions: Check guidebooks to attorneys such as the *Martindale-Hubble Law Directory* (www.martindale.com), available in the reference section of most larger public libraries. And don't forget the yellow pages of your local telephone books.

4. Investigate costs and fee structure. Once you've found an attorney who concentrates in estate planning, the first question you probably have is, "How much is this going to cost me?"

That's a fair question. If the price is too high, it's best to find out as soon as possible and look for someone else. But most people have no clear idea how much the lawyer's services should cost them, and I don't have an easy answer. Since everyone's situation is different, and prices differ from region to region, the price that's "appropriate" can vary tremendously.

To give you a feel for what to expect, however, an average person in need of a plain-vanilla estate plan including the standard documents should expect to pay anywhere from $500 to $3,000. On the other hand, multimillion-dollar estates requiring complex estate-planning tools might reasonably cost $5,000 to $15,000 and much more. Such plans can save these estates millions of dollars in taxes.

Don't assume you'll receive inadequate service from a lower-cost attorney. Many competent attorneys specializing in estate planning have modest offices and low overhead. Many of these lawyers will do a great job for you at a reasonable price, particularly if there's nothing very unusual about your situation. Besides, not everyone is comfortable in fancy or pretentious law firm suites.

Most estate-planning lawyers, even the most expensive ones, offer a free consultation for prospective clients. Before your get-acquainted interview or initial consultation, confirm that this first meeting is conducted at no charge.

Before agreeing to anything, you should ask the attorney for an estimated cost for the whole job. Otherwise everyone's time can be wasted and misunderstandings could result. Beyond the lawyer's hourly rate, you have a right to know up front how much your whole estate plan will cost, even if it is just an estimated range. Let the lawyer take a look at the information you've brought with you concerning your assets and your personal and family situation. That should help him estimate what your plan will require.

The cost of your estate plan may vary according to the amount of time the lawyer will spend on it. Many lawyers will charge a flat fee for drafting the documents and for advising you generally as to how your various assets should be structured, if restructuring is needed to avoid probate or reduce future estate taxes.

If you want the attorney involved in all aspects of that restructuring, such as filling out change-of-ownership or change-of-beneficiary forms, this will naturally add to the time and increase the cost of the estate plan.

There's a growing trend for lawyers to charge a flat fee for estate planning, in which case you might get a fairly precise quote, but make sure that everything you will need for a complete plan is included in this fee. Some attorneys offer a flat fee for services that include only the barest bones, with many other components being added to the bill. After reading this book, you should have a good idea what components your plan will require. After being quoted a fee, don't be afraid to ask for a discount, especially if you expect that your plan will be relatively simple and without any twists.

5. Size up a lawyer. The initial consultation offers you an opportunity to assess the attorney's personality, competence, and communication skills. Don't underestimate the importance of personality. Find someone with whom you can work efficiently, someone with whom you're comfortable discussing very intimate details of your family and finances. If you don't feel you click with a particular attorney, that can be a very good reason to look for someone else.

Here are some other questions to ask yourself after your first meeting:

Question:	Yes	No	Your comments
Did she return your telephone call promptly?			
Did she listen to what you had to say, and communicate her own thoughts in a manner that you were able to understand?			
Did she make you wait beyond the scheduled appointment time?			
How long has she been an estate-planning attorney?			
Can she provide references—both other lawyers and clients?			

Also consider calling your state bar to ask if any complaints have been filed against this attorney, or whether she has ever been disciplined by the bar.

Some estate-planning attorneys belong to national marketing networks, which usually provide their own form documents to the attorney. Some of these networks are better than others. If you retain an attorney who is part of a national network, keep an eye out for two factors:

- First, since the network is likely to be national in scope, make certain the documents are not overly voluminous, in an attempt to comply with the laws of all states. You can ask to take a look at a sample set of documents to see how much extraneous material (items not applicable to the state in which you live) is included.

- Second, make sure you are dealing directly with the attorney who is writing the documents. Many financial planners take an interest in a client's complete financial picture and are involved in estate-planning aspects in a very positive way. But some financial planners position themselves as go-betweens, so that you may not even meet with a lawyer. What that does is add another layer of fees. Fee splitting between estate-planning lawyers and financial planners is prohibited in most states, but it is still prevalent in some circles.

Once you've made a decision, here's what to expect: Typically, in a relatively simple situation, an estate-planning attorney might meet with you once or twice before signing documents, in addition to your initial consultation. Expect each meeting to last between one and three hours or more, depending on the complexity of the plan, your personal concerns, and the attorney's level of detail in explanation. Ask all your questions. There is no such thing as a stupid question!

At the first meeting, you'll likely discuss your estate and intentions; at the second, you'll probably review a draft of the estate plan and sign it; or you might have a third meeting to sign the documents. Of course, if you have a very complex plan, more meetings will be required.

As a reminder, here are the goals for your estate plan:
- to hold and ultimately dispose of your assets and provide for anybody dependent upon you
- to transfer your assets, upon your death, to the persons or charities you've selected, under the conditions you've chosen, while minimizing extraneous costs such as probate and estate taxes

A complete estate plan usually consists of these documents:

1. revocable living trust
2. will (a "pour-over will" if used in conjunction with a revocable living trust)
3. power of attorney for property
4. health care directives (power of attorney for health care and perhaps a living will)
5. other documents—such as real estate deeds—that implement the plan

Your estate-plan documents might be augmented by charitable or insurance trusts, gifting programs, or other advanced techniques. We'll take a look at some of the key weapons of the estate-planning arsenal shortly.

Once you begin the process, your lawyer should continue to provide you with the attention that you received initially. Does she still return your telephone calls promptly? The number one reason people become dissatisfied with their lawyers and other service professionals is their failure to return telephone calls.

Some lawyers, being human, also procrastinate. If you feel your lawyer is not working diligently toward finishing your estate plan after beginning the process, communicate this to her, and if necessary begin the process again with a new lawyer.

Estate planning is often more art than exact science, because personalities and family dynamics are so important to estate planning. Five different lawyers may have five different approaches to the same situation, all of which may be valid. Even the same lawyer's work will evolve, so that the documents a lawyer might have prepared five years ago are different in various aspects than those drafted now. This does not make the old documents bad, but laws obviously change, and in many cases a lawyer may learn a few things on the practice road that will "tweak" documents for the better.

Action Plan Four: Let's Keep the Ball Rolling!

A five-step strategy for selecting your attorney:

1. *Today,* call trusted friends and ask whether they can recommend an estate-planning attorney.

2. If your friends can't help, *by the end of the week* find an attorney through a referral from another professional, such as your CPA, banker, or insurance broker; or use a referral service, such as the state or local bar association.

3. Call the attorney (or attorneys) next *Monday* and do a very brief preliminary interview. Does he concentrate his practice on estate planning? Does he offer a free initial consultation? Is his cost structure reasonable? Can he schedule a consultation at a time that fits your schedule?

4. Book an appointment and *write it in your calendar.* Make arrangements for child care (or bring your children, if it's okay with both you and the lawyer) or get some time off work if necessary.

5. *Between now and then,* complete this book so you're as prepared as possible.

CHAPTER 5

Looking out for Yourself (Avoiding an Adult Guardianship)

"Even if you're on the right track, you'll get run over if you just sit there."

—Will Rogers

Many people start the estate-planning process with their families in mind, thinking that all they need is a "simple" will so that their assets will be divided properly after their death. Others want to explore the potential for reducing possibly onerous estate taxes.

But most people don't realize just how much an estate plan can do for them while they're still alive—if they would just stop procrastinating and get the plan done.

Generally speaking, a well-crafted estate plan can benefit you during your lifetime in two ways: It can speak for you on matters of health care and finance when you are incapacitated and therefore unable to speak for yourself; it can protect your assets against lawsuits and other threats.

If you've been procrastinating about estate planning because you feel so young and vital, look at it in another way: as a way to be prepared for the unexpected. A properly constructed estate plan can make a big difference if you:

- have a serious accident, stroke, or other misfortune that leaves you unable to look after your own assets
- need to have a medical decision made during an operation while you're under anesthesia
- develop a medical condition that leaves you unable to convey your wishes about your place of residence or medical care, or
- have a hopeless medical condition and would like your opinion heard about the efforts made to keep you alive

Let's examine those events and see what a well-crafted estate plan can do for you now—while you're still alive.

Guardianship of the Person

If you become incapacitated and are unable to speak for yourself, and you don't have the proper documents in place, there's a strong chance your medical care will be handled differently than you would want. Other people will be making life-and-death decisions for you, without the benefit of your input.

In this case, your family will be forced to go into court and initiate a "living probate"* known as a guardianship or a conservatorship.

The court will appoint a "guardian of the person" with respect to your health care matters (and a "guardian for the estate" to handle your financial affairs, which we'll cover a little later). In a guardianship of the person proceeding, the court appoints a guardian to make health care and lifestyle decisions for you if you

---

*When most people think of probate, they think of what is more specifically known as "death probate," the mechanism for transferring assets from a deceased person to his heirs. And indeed the term "probate" originally referred exclusively to a court procedure used to validate or invalidate a will and determine heirship. The meaning of "probate" has expanded over the years to include all the activities of the probate court.

can no longer effectively communicate. For example, the court typically grants its appointed guardian authority to select a place of residence for you, which may mean a nursing home.

So if probate is available to those who don't plan ahead, why bother with estate planning? Easy: If you have an estate plan, *you* get to select your guardian and *you* provide guidelines or instructions to follow in case you become incapacitated.

The biggest problem with probate, however, is the cost in time and money. When a person without a power of attorney for health care is kept alive in a hospital by life-sustaining machines, the family's decision to curtail such care might not be accepted until the family works its way through the time-consuming, potentially costly, and possibly embarrassing probate court process to name a guardian. While some circumstances may allow for a quick guardianship resolution, others may drag on for years, especially if family members cannot agree on a course of action. Meanwhile, depending on your health insurance, hospital bills might be piling up alongside the legal bills.

Health Care Directives

Fortunately, there are estate-planning tools, known as "health care directives" or "advance directives," to ensure that even if you are unable to communicate, your philosophies regarding life-and-death decisions will be implemented. The most widely recognized health care directives are:

- powers of attorney for health care, which state your wishes *and* appoint someone to make choices regarding your treatment
- living wills, which simply state your wishes regarding treatment

Both are based on the idea that adults have the absolute right to make their own medical care decisions. This includes the decision to have life-sustaining procedures withheld or withdrawn and to be able to delegate the execution of that decision to others.

The right to die is controversial, replete with ethical, moral, religious, and legal issues. You probably have some feeling about how *you* would like your situation to be handled if you had a terminal medical condition.

Many times, when a crucial medical issue arises, the person with the most at stake—the patient—is unable to communicate intelligently. By signing a health care directive before incompetence becomes an issue, you are not relinquishing any immediate control. As long as you are competent to direct the physician, you speak for yourself. If at some later point you are unable to communicate or are judged incompetent, you'll still guide your family and physician through your health care directive.

It's possible that even without health care directives, your family and physician will be able to navigate an acceptable course of action for your care if it becomes necessary. They might even make the same choices you would. However, without health care directives, there is no guarantee. Unique circumstances, the personalities of family members, or the philosophy of the physician or even a hospital administrator can become a factor in what are literally life-and-death matters. When this happens, your fate is in question and your family is dragged through what can be an extremely painful and expensive process that can take on a life of its own.

A federal law known as the Patient Self-Determination Act requires hospitals, nursing homes, and other medical institutions that receive federal funding to inform patients of their right to execute health care directives. However, there is no law requiring patients to follow through. It's still up to you to decide to get it done.

Power of Attorney for Health Care

A power of attorney for health care is usually more important than a living will. It is provided for by statute in most states and may be referred to as a Statutory Short Form Power of Attorney for Health Care. This document allows you to express your philosophy regarding life-sustaining procedures and lets you appoint an agent (also called a "proxy" or "surrogate") to make your health care decisions for you when you are unable to do so.

Your agent can be any competent adult except, in most states, your own treating physician. (If a relative of yours happens to be a physician, but not your personal physician, you can choose that person as your agent.)

Generally speaking, the best choices are close and trusted loved ones, particularly if they live nearby. You should name a primary agent and, in case that person is unable to act, additional agents listed consecutively in the document. Selecting an agent can be a difficult decision, but it's better to make a tough or imperfect choice than to do nothing.

FUN FACT

In some states if you select your spouse as your health care agent and later get divorced, his or her appointment is considered automatically revoked unless it is renewed after the divorce. The legislature figures that nobody wants an ex-spouse empowered to come running into the hospital to "pull the plug."

You can make a power of attorney for health care effective immediately or at some time in the future, such as "when I am unable to make decisions on my own behalf and my attending physician and agent so certify to this condition." Don't worry that you're signing away your free will; as long as you, the principal, can articulate your wishes regarding health care decisions, you still have unquestioned authority over your own medical care.

You can direct your agent to act on your behalf in any manner you choose. The Illinois Statutory Power of Attorney for

Health Care offers three varying statements of philosophy about life-sustaining treatment from which to choose. These statements, listed below, can be used as templates, or you can write something of your own design.

1. I do not want my life to be prolonged nor do I want life-sustaining treatment to be provided or continued if my agent believes the burdens of the treatment outweigh the expected benefits. I want my agent to consider the relief of suffering, the expense involved, and the quality as well as the possible extension of my life in making decisions concerning life-sustaining treatment. (Note: Some of my clients take "expense" out of the equation entirely because they believe the maintenance cost should not be a factor.)

2. I want my life to be prolonged and I want life-sustaining treatment to be provided or continued unless I am in a coma that my attending physician believes to be irreversible, in accordance with reasonable medical standards at the time of reference. If and when I have suffered irreversible coma, I want life-sustaining treatment to be withheld or discontinued. (Note: You may feel more comfortable by adding the requirement that at least one other unaffiliated licensed physician must certify as to your condition.)

3. I want my life to be prolonged to the greatest extent possible without regard to my condition, the chances I have for recovery, or the cost of the procedures. (Note: a.k.a. the cryonics option.)

Unless specifically limited, most statutory powers of attorney for health care give your agent the authority to make any decision regarding your medical care you would be able to make if capable of communicating your wishes.

A power of attorney for health care can even grant authority to withhold nutrients and hydration (food and water). If you do not want to be left in a prolonged coma with no hope of recovery, instructions to withhold food and water, in a humane manner, might be the only way to have your wishes granted. Withholding food and water is not possible with just a living will.

Your agent's authority can be limited in any fashion you wish, including but not limited to the listing of any medical procedures that you find abhorrent. You may insist on:

- no electrical or mechanical resuscitation of the heart when it has stopped beating
- no nasogastric (feeding-tube) feeding when paralyzed or unable to take nourishment by mouth
- no mechanical respiration when unable to sustain breathing

Limits may be placed on the power to make an anatomical gift or to authorize an autopsy and specify when to make every attempt to resuscitate and when not to intervene.

In order to properly execute a power of attorney for health care, you must sign the document in the presence of at least one witness who is neither an heir nor your treating physician. Some states require a second witness and/or a notary's seal.

After you have executed the power of attorney for health care, you should give copies of it to your physician and others associated with your health care, such as a nursing home or other facility. Ask them to make it a permanent part of your medical file. This way, even if your family cannot find a copy of the document in an emergency, your medical provider should have it on hand.

Surrogate Acts

Many states have what are known as Surrogate Acts, which apply in the event of a terminal illness or a hopeless condition. These direct that if you have not executed a power of attorney for health care, your health care provider can select a person to act as agent on your behalf, in the event that you become unable to speak for yourself.

Every competent adult would be better off executing a power of attorney for health care and selecting an agent of choice rather than allowing a hospital or physician to make that selection.

Without a power of attorney for health care, the "wrong" person is particularly likely to be selected to speak for you if:

- you have a longtime partner to whom you are not married
- you are married, but are separated or otherwise not on good terms with your spouse
- you have at least one child who does not know of your wishes
- your parents are still alive, but you have not discussed the matter with them
- you are married but have children from a previous marriage, especially if they don't have a good relationship with your new spouse or have philosophical differences with him or her over matters relating to your health care
- your closest relatives have religious views you do not share, or you have religious views they do not share, leading to a disagreement over philosophy about life-and-death decisions
- you have no close family

REAL-LIFE STORIES

Phil had a twenty-five-year relationship with a partner of the same sex, and had recently become incapacitated with a serious medical condition that rendered him unable to communicate. Phil's family did not approve of his lifestyle, and excluded his partner from all decision making, instead taking charge themselves even though the family had been estranged from

REAL-LIFE STORIES

Phil and they had not even spoken for years. Those in long-standing same-sex relationships must realize that unless they live in a state such as Vermont that legally recognizes gay marriage, their relationship will have no legal standing when it comes to naming an agent. For those who plan ahead, however, many of these problems are easily overcome.

Sometimes people learn the importance of a power of attorney for health care the hard way. Vivian, 68, had to undergo a serious surgical procedure a year ago. When she awoke in the hospital after the operation, she was given some bad news: While the operation had been a success, a second operation would be necessary. The surgeon had discovered an additional condition during the first operation, but without Vivian's consent, he was not legally able to address that problem. An agent under a power of attorney for health care could have provided that consent and saved Vivian from a second surgery. Before the second procedure, Vivian put a power of attorney for health care in place, selecting an agent who could make decisions during the time that she couldn't.

The Living Will

Almost every state has a living will statute that allows an individual, officially known as the declarant, to state that he does not wish to be kept alive by extraordinary medical procedures.

While the power of attorney for health care is an *action* document that relates to any medical decision, the living will is a *static* document describing your philosophy regarding "pull-the-plug" decisions. A living will becomes effective less often than a power of attorney for health care; moreover, the power of attorney for health care takes precedence over a living will whenever the agent named in the power is available. Still, it may be a good idea to have a living will as well as a power of attorney for health care in case your agent is not available, or to make your wishes crystal clear (provided, of course, that the documents do not conflict with each other).

If after signing a living will you become unable to communicate due to accident or illness, the living will speaks for you. The physician is then authorized by the document itself to withhold or withdraw life-sustaining procedures within a limited set of circumstances without risk of incurring liability for that act.

The living will becomes effective *only* in a very specific situation: when the declarant is unable to communicate *and* has a terminal condition. In such a case, the physician is instructed not to provide care that will only delay dying. Care that serves another purpose, such as reducing pain or offering a possible cure, can still be administered.

An Example of a Living Will

The relevant portions of a typical state living will statute read:

"I, Janet Doe, being of sound mind, willfully and voluntarily make known my desire that my moment of death shall not be artificially postponed under the circumstances set forth below, and do hereby declare:

"If at any time I should have an incurable and irreversible injury, disease, or illness judged to be a terminal condition by my attending physician, who has personally examined me and has determined that my death is imminent except for death-delaying procedures, I direct that such procedures that would only prolong the dying process be withheld or withdrawn, and that I be permitted to die naturally with only the administration of medication, sustenance, or the performance of any medical procedure deemed necessary by my attending physician to provide me with comfort care.

"In addition, I direct that such death-delaying procedures be withheld or withdrawn if there is no reasonable expectation of my recovery from physical or mental disability. I ask that drugs be mercifully administered to me for terminal suffering, even if they hasten the moment of my death.

"In the absence of my ability to give directions regarding the use of such death-delaying procedures, it is my intention that this declaration shall be honored by my family and physician as the final expression of my legal right to refuse medical or surgical treatment and accept the consequences from such refusal."

Since the living will is simply a statement of philosophy, you may modify it with any language that you feel more accurately reflects your own thoughts. You might use different philosophical guidelines and instructions. Refer to page 61 on the power of attorney for health care to give you an idea on where you might draw the line regarding various medical procedures.

The problem is that it's almost impossible to prepare for every contingency. Rather than attempting to list every last situation in a living will, make your power of attorney for health care as detailed as you wish and trust your agent to cover unforeseen occurrences.

A living will must be dated, signed, and witnessed by two competent adults who are not heirs. Although not necessarily required, it is probably good practice to notarize the document as well.

REAL-LIFE STORIES

Two grown sisters, Sally, 34, and Jennifer, 32, were informed that their father, Paul, 71, was in a coma in a Chicago-area hospital. Jennifer had cared for him the past ten years, and

REAL-LIFE STORIES

knew his philosophy regarding being kept alive when there was no hope of recovery and prospects of an extremely poor quality of life. Paul had made it a point to discuss the matter with Jennifer because he had been in failing health for years. However, he had delayed making his wishes official through the proper estate-planning documents.

Per Paul's earlier request, Jennifer asked to have her father's life support disconnected. Sally did not agree. She had had little to do with her father's care, having moved to Oregon years before, but she came back when Paul entered the hospital.

Sally insisted that Paul's life support be maintained. Perhaps she was feeling guilty about the fact that she'd been away so long. Perhaps her personal philosophy was that any human life should always be maintained. Perhaps it was a matter of sibling rivalry, and as the older sister, she wanted to maintain the dominance she had had when both were children. Whatever the reason, Paul's failure to document his personal philosophy and to choose a daughter as his agent for making health care decisions created family strife and prolonged his life against his wishes, while his savings were depleted by hospital bills and legal costs from the guardianship battle.

HOW TO DEFEAT PROCRASTINATION

If you're procrastinating out of fear, you can help eliminate the fear by getting more information.

As you fill in the blanks about what you need to do, what's missing, and how to handle the task, your fear will decrease and you will be able to get started.

Do-Not-Resuscitate Orders (DNRs)

Unfortunately, health care directives are not always honored by hospitals, physicians, or paramedics. The final document needed to prevent unwanted last-minute medical heroics is a DNR, or "Do Not Resuscitate" order, which can be issued only by an attending physician upon request from a patient or the patient's designated health care agent. DNRs are very common in intensive-care wards and are the final word on life-sustaining treatment. But a doctor will not issue a DNR unless a person is already very ill—you can't just ask your doctor to fill one out as a precaution while you're still fit. If a DNR has been issued, it should be posted prominently near the patient's bed or in her home.

It's a fairly safe bet that physicians and other hospital workers will honor a DNR order. But in certain states, such as New York, paramedics and other ambulance personnel summoned to provide care outside of a hospital setting are required by law to attempt to prolong life despite a prominently posted DNR.

Organ Donation

Many states actively promote programs where drivers indicate consent on the backs of their driver's licenses to make anatomical gifts, under whatever restrictions the driver wishes to impose.

A power of attorney for health care is another critical place to state your intentions regarding organ donation or authorizing any other means of anatomical gifts. In fact, many of the statutory powers of attorney for health care forms contain a section devoted to this subject, where you can permit your agent to donate any organ or specify certain organs for donation. To ensure that your intentions are followed, you should have your preferences for organ donation explained on both your driver's license and health care power of attorney. In addition, you should make your wishes known to your family.

For those who have not given the matter much thought, consider that many thousands of people suffer needlessly or even die each year for lack of donor organs. Especially needed are young donors, since their organs tend to be more robust. Unfortunately, many young people don't bother with organ-donor arrangements, since they feel that death is so distant. But accidents happen. Through organ donation, even a senseless death might come to have some meaning.

Guardianship of the Estate

Failure to plan for the possibility of becoming temporarily or permanently unable to perform financial transactions can lead to another type of living probate known as guardianship of the estate. As with guardianship of the person, guardianship of the estate requires your family to go through a court proceeding to appoint a guardian to act on your behalf to handle your finances, such as signing your checks in order to pay bills.

The way to avoid this form of probate is by executing a durable power of attorney for property while you are still competent to make your own decisions. This is in many ways similar to the power of attorney for health care. With such an arrangement, you appoint an agent to perform financial transactions on your behalf when you become unable to do so.

Perhaps as a reflection of our aging population, probate courts today are crowded with people seeking the appointment of guardians to perform financial transactions for older, incompetent individuals. As a result, legislatures throughout the country have enacted statutes providing for a durable power of attorney for property in order to avoid such court proceedings.

The document is relatively simple; it allows you to select a trusted agent to handle your financial transactions during any period of your disability or incompetence without the necessity of petitioning the probate court for formal guardianship of your estate.

This can be a vital tool if you become incapacitated and you need someone to handle necessary or time-sensitive financial transactions. (Even if you already have a trust with a named successor trustee, you should have a durable power of attorney for property as well, since a trustee is able to handle only transactions involving assets that are in the trust.) For example, you might need someone to:

- transfer an asset from your personal estate into a trust
- act on your behalf with respect to a joint tenancy asset
- go into your safe-deposit box
- sign and file your tax return
- pay your rent or mortgage
- pay insurance premiums or make a claim
- renew a certificate of deposit that has matured in your IRA
- make gifts qualifying for the Annual Exclusion

The durable power of attorney for property grants your agent the power to act within the parameters that you create. You choose whether the document becomes effective when it's signed or at some future date, such as when your primary physician concludes, in writing, that you are unable to manage your financial transactions. The durable power of attorney for property also can end at any time you dictate, such as when you regain your senses, but it always ends upon your death. A delicate dance is required to make sure the durable power of attorney for property is usable when it is needed, but not subject to abuse prior to or even after it is needed.

Here is an example of language that demonstrates your desire for your family to act under a power of attorney for property on your behalf, but only at some time in the future: "This power of attorney shall become effective when my spouse, living and competent (or if my spouse is not living or not competent, when a majority of my children who are living and competent), certifies in writing along with my attending physician, who has personally examined me, that in their judgment I am unable properly to manage my financial affairs."

For a durable power of attorney to be official, you must sign it while you are competent. It must also be notarized, which means that a notary must be present to attest to your signature as the principal. In many states an independent witness must also attest to your signature.

Durable versus Nondurable Power of Attorney

A nondurable power of attorney is designed to serve a specific purpose and then end. It also automatically ends if you die or become incompetent. A nondurable power of attorney may be general or limited. A general power of attorney may be used when one party is representing another in negotiations. A limited power of attorney is most often used for a specific transaction, such as when you are unable to be physically present to sign documents or handle a certain transaction. For example, if you are party to a real estate closing and are unable to be present at the closing, you would give someone a limited power of attorney, which is effective for a set period of time and relates only to that transaction. If the principal of a nondurable general or limited power of attorney becomes incompetent, the agent's authority will end.

A durable power of attorney, on the other hand, is called "durable" because it survives any subsequent disability or incompetence. It was created to enable you to plan for such a possibility.

Differences between a durable power of attorney and a non-durable power of attorney (whether general or limited):

Durable Power of Attorney	Nondurable Power of Attorney (Limited or General)
Its purpose is to allow a person to act on your behalf with respect to financial transactions if you become incapacitated.	Its purpose is to allow a person to act on your behalf with respect to some specific financial transaction or series of transactions.
Survives subsequent incapacity.	Ends if you become incapacitated.
Acts with respect to a wide range of transactions under any parameters you've set.	Relates only to a specific transaction or series of transactions.
Effective either when it's signed or at some future date or triggering event, such as when selected parties determine you are unable to conduct business transactions.	Usually limited for a set period of time and until a specific transaction is completed, or is ongoing based upon various business factors.
Ends at any time you dictate, usually when you regain your ability to conduct business transactions.	Ends at any time you dictate, usually when a specific transaction is completed or a business relationship changes.

All powers of attorney, whether durable or not, must be signed by you while you are competent and should be notarized. Requirement of an independent witness varies from state to state. All financial powers of attorney, whether they are durable or general, terminate upon your death.

Another useful tool in avoiding guardianship over your estate is establishing and fully funding a revocable living trust (also called a revocable trust or a living trust). (See chapter 8 for a complete discussion of revocable living trusts.)

Action Plan Five: Don't Stop Now!

A five-step strategy to prepare for your own incapacity:

1. *Today*, take a moment to consider how you would like your health care to be handled if your chances for recovery are slim and you are unable to communicate. Put your thoughts into writing.

2. If your thoughts on these matters are not clear, speak to people you trust. Ask your doctor for her advice, or ask people you know who have been through extensive medical procedures themselves.

3. *Over the next week*, decide who would best represent your health care interests if you were incapacitated. Is there a close friend or relative whose judgment you trust? Is this person likely to be available when needed? Discuss with your prospective agent your philosophy on sustaining or ending your life if you are in a hopeless medical condition. Would he or she be willing to act according to your wishes?

4. If you have special circumstances, such as a divisive relationship among your relatives, plan to minimize any potential disharmony. One example is when there is bad blood between your current spouse and your grown children from a previous marriage. If you believe that there may be conflict regarding your care, it is important to be very specific about delegating the proper authority to be exercised under certain conditions.

5. Draft your own living will. This isn't entirely necessary, but it will help you get your thoughts on the subject in order. You can have this document reviewed by your estate-planning attorney when you meet. Even if the attorney thinks it best to redo the wording or its form, having your thoughts down on paper is an efficient way to begin.

6. Relax; take a break. You have made terrific progress in completing your estate plan!

CHAPTER 6

Protecting Your Assets While You're Around to Enjoy Them

"I'm not dead (yet)."
—Unfortunate peasant protesting that he is not ready to
be carted away, in *Monty Python and the Holy Grail*

Estate planning can help you protect your estate from those who would like to grab it from you. However, there are many nuances involved in sufficiently armoring yourself. As a result, there are whole books devoted to this topic, so if you are losing sleep at night worrying about your liabilities, read this chapter and then go buy a more specialized treatment of the subject.

The Threat of Lawsuits

Suing people seems to have replaced baseball as our national pastime. Thousands of lawsuits are filed every day in this country. Many people lose sleep over the threat of a lawsuit—and many of those who don't would if they realized how little it would take for them to lose everything they own.

Members of professions that are at particularly high risk for lawsuits, such as physicians or, ironically, lawyers, have additional reason to be obsessed with potential liabilities, although every American is a potential victim. Are the lawyers to blame for the explosion of lawsuits? Certainly the contingency-fee arrangement, in which an attorney is paid a percentage of the amount collected (often 33 percent or more), is a factor.

But lawyers can also be a solution—estate-planning lawyers, anyway, because it is possible to protect yourself through estate planning. Lawsuit protection (also commonly referred to as asset protection) has a place in this book only because the tools often used are estate-planning tools, and can be arranged by estate-planning lawyers. But protecting your assets during your life is also a way to ensure that they'll be there after your death, for your heirs.

Let's say you are driving late at night and hit another car from behind. You didn't see the other car because it was very dark and the other car had no brakelights. You exchange insurance information and learn the following week that the other person (the plaintiff) has hired a lawyer. The plaintiff claims to have suffered a personal injury. You have auto insurance, but the plaintiff asks for more money than your insurance policy limits (the maximum amount your insurance company can be obligated to pay).

If the lawsuit results in a judgment greater than the amount your insurance will cover, that makes it a subject for estate planning. This isn't too unusual; juries are often more than willing to throw around other people's money like confetti.

At this point, the plaintiff may go after your personal assets. First, depending on the size of the judgment, virtually all of your assets could be seized or have liens placed upon them—liens that must be satisfied before you can pocket any money when the assets are sold. Next, if the plaintiff's damages still are not paid, your future earnings could be garnished. While the plaintiff turns his attention to suing the manufacturer of the car he was driving, or the city where the accident happened, you're left with next to nothing.

Assessing Your Risk of Losing
Assets in a Lawsuit

Not everyone is at the same risk of losing his or her assets in a lawsuit. High-risk groups include:

- physicians, lawyers, and certain small-business owners
- people with minimal liability coverage on their auto or homeowner's insurance
- those who own assets together with other people. For example, if you own your house in joint tenancy (discussed in more detail in chapter 8), you could lose it if the other joint owner is successfully sued. Partnership and corporate assets can also be lost to a plaintiff's claim against your partner or corporate associate or because of the negligence of your partner or an employee.
- the rich and famous. They make appealing targets for lawsuits, frivolous and otherwise.

HOW TO DEFEAT PROCRASTINATION

If you're just not in the mood, ask yourself, "Is there anything—any part of this task—I'd be willing to do right now?"

Find something. Anything. And do it.

It doesn't have to be related to the task—you just need to get your motor running. Once you're busy, you'll find it's easier to switch gears and get to the important task at hand.

Protecting Personal Assets

Protecting personal assets from lawsuits is a complex subject, and certainly anyone with an extremely large estate to protect, or with some other reason to believe she is likely to be the victim of a lawsuit, might decide to consult a specialist.

Here are a few simple strategies to minimize your risk.

Strategy 1: Purchasing Insurance

Almost everyone with a house or a car has homeowner's and automobile insurance policies. If you have a mortgage on your house, your lender will mandate homeowner's insurance. Auto liability insurance is required of drivers in most states. But those who rent their homes are often lax about purchasing renter's insurance, typically a low-cost form of insurance that can protect against both lawsuits and theft.

Many people fail to take advantage of umbrella coverage. Umbrella policies can be extremely useful in filling in gaps in other insurance policies when it comes to liability. For just a few hundred dollars a year or less, you can add millions of dollars of liability protection to your existing coverage. If you don't have an umbrella policy, ask your home and auto insurance providers if it's something they offer. If you have a job that carries the risk of a lawsuit, you also need professional liability or errors-and-omissions insurance, and if you own a small business, you may need more insurance to protect you from various potential liabilities.

Strategy 2: Incorporation

Forming a corporation is a common and effective method of protecting personal assets from business-related liabilities. But incorporating should not be viewed as the ultimate protection. The shield that the corporation offers from personal liability can be defeated. This is commonly referred to by lawyers as "piercing the corporate veil."

How can this happen? If you incorporate, your personal assets should be protected from acts of negligence by your employees, but what if you are personally negligent? The law mandates that a corporation and its principals comply with many different rules and regulations, so it can be easy to unintentionally violate one of these rules or regulations.

Under many circumstances, your personal assets can be used to satisfy an outstanding corporate liability. Even if an employee other than yourself acted negligently, all kinds of theories can be bootstrapped to lay the ultimate negligence at your personal doorstep.

Strategy 3: Forming a Limited Partnership or Limited Liability Company

Forming a limited partnership (LP) or limited liability company (LLC) is also a common and effective method of protecting personal assets from various types of liabilities. Let's say that you own a building and are afraid that someone might injure himself on the premises. Creditors of a limited partner or a member of an LLC generally cannot reach LP or LLC assets or force their way into the LP or LLC business. While a creditor might be able to obtain the right to receive a partner's or member's share of distributions from the LP or LLC, if the entity makes no distributions, the assets are protected from his creditors.

An advantage of the LLC over the LP is that a member of an LLC may not have put his personal assets (those not owned by the LLC) at risk in the case of a liability, whereas the general partner of an LP may have his personal assets at risk. One way that the general partner of an LP can protect personal assets is to make the general partner of the LP a corporation, which is then owned by the individual. This adds complexity that is not necessary when using an LLC and is one reason that LLCs are gaining in popularity over LPs.

A type of LP known as a family limited partnership (FLP) and a type of LLC known as a family limited liability company

(FLLC) can serve as handy asset-protection tools while serving various estate planning needs as well. We'll consider FLPs and FLLCs more in Chapter 12.

Revocable Trusts versus Prenuptial Agreements

Revocable trusts can be used to help protect your assets in case of a divorce. Let's say you're a reasonably successful person about to get married. Do you ask your spouse-to-be for a prenuptial agreement?

Most people cringe at the thought of raising the topic and putting the nascent relationship at risk, but what about the possibility of losing half your assets? Revocable trusts can provide a partial solution, helping ensure that your assets will remain your assets in the event of a divorce.

Before you wed, all of your major personal assets are placed in a trust. Precise bookkeeping is crucial to doing this correctly. These trust assets, which you accumulated prior to marriage, must be kept segregated from those you acquire after the marriage. Assets that are mixed with those of your newly beloved are at increased risk in a divorce. Assets can be removed from your preestablished trust if you so choose, but after the wedding, new assets cannot be moved into it. This is not a foolproof method for protecting assets—in truth, neither is a prenuptial agreement—but it's a solid tool.

It's also less inflammatory than a prenuptial agreement because:

- you don't have to get a signature from your future spouse; you don't even have to mention that you have a trust or that assets have been transferred to it
- you avoid the use of the hot-button term "prenup," which carries all sorts of baggage with it

- you can avoid disclosing to your spouse *all* of your assets, something that is *required* for a valid prenuptial

Action Plan Six: You're Getting There!

A five-step plan to reduce risks to your estate:

1. *Today*, consider your risk of liability. Is there any particular reason to believe you could become the target of a lawsuit? Are you in an occupation in which you may be sued because of your work?

2. *Over the next few days*, check your insurance policies—auto, home, business—to determine how much liability coverage you actually have.

3. *Within the next week*, discuss your liability coverage with your insurance agent and, if appropriate, plug the gaps. Do you have umbrella insurance?

4. Review the estate-planning tools that might offer you some lawsuit protection and discuss them with your attorney.

5. If you are planning to get married, think about the possibility of divorce. I know—you're not going into marriage expecting to get divorced, but it doesn't hurt to take steps to protect your assets. Improper planning may result in your losing substantially more assets in a divorce than would otherwise be the case.

CHAPTER 7

The Cost of Death Probate and Ways to Avoid It

"Being of sound mind, I spent it all."
—Leon Jaworski, referring to the shortest will on record

Do you care about your family? Of course you do. Procrastinate about estate planning, and it's your family who suffers. They might face considerable delays, sizable legal costs, and taxes, too. It's possible to protect your family from the worst of these, but doing so requires proper utilization of the estate-planning tools at your disposal.

Some of the concepts involved in this process can be a bit complex or at least unpleasant to think about. But remember, that's why you're working with an estate-planning attorney. The message of this chapter is straightforward: Use trusts. For those wanting to look after their families, trusts of various shapes and sizes will play a key role. But before we get to trusts, we'll consider what may happen with your estate if you fail to prepare properly.

Death Probate

We've already discussed two forms of living probate—guardianships of the estate and guardianships of the person.

These are avoidable with durable powers of attorney for property and health care.

In this chapter, we turn to death probate, the more familiar form of probate that occurs at death. Death probate is not a punishment that the government dreamed up to inflict upon grieving families, even if it does sometimes seem that way. The probate court was established under British common law to provide a mechanism for beneficiaries to obtain clear and absolute ownership of an asset after the previous owner has died. It is, in effect, a lawsuit brought by heirs against potential creditors and other claimants, establishing the person or entity that controls the administration process (the executor) and eventually cutting off any claims, so that title to assets is clear and no future claims will be recognized.

Before title to an asset can be transferred to an heir, the probate court must ensure that all bills and claims against the deceased's estate are paid and that other safeguards are taken to ensure that the assets are transferred to the proper beneficiaries.

In this process, the executor of the estate (the administrator, if the individual died without a will) gathers the assets of the testator (the deceased person), pays any debts and taxes, notifies heirs, and eventually distributes whatever is left to the beneficiaries, per your directions if you left a will or per the laws of intestate succession if you didn't. (See the state survey #1) Probate rules vary from state to state, but all require that assets remain in the estate for some minimum period of time, often around six months, so that any creditors have time to assert their claims against those assets.

Since probate involves going to court—that is, a public forum in which lawsuits are brought—it tends to increase the chances that your estate plan will be contested.

Typical issues in will contests include:

- the competency of the deceased when the will was signed
- improper execution of the will

- duress or undue influence by another person
- inadequate consideration to a surviving spouse (see chapter 11)

If a will is contested, the drain of assets from legal fees and other expenses from the estate can be enormous. Your risk can be reduced greatly through the use of a revocable trust. In most states, revocable trusts are signed with much less formality than wills, and they're less likely to be subject to attack on technical grounds.

As you will see in the next chapter, the best weapon for avoiding probate can be the revocable trust.

FUN FACT—OR FICTION?

It is a popular belief that the word "testator," like "testify," derives from the fact that long ago, in feudal times, oaths were sworn while gripping one's "family jewels." However, scholars say the words actually derive from the Latin "testi," meaning witness.

The Cost of Probate

Most families hire a lawyer to probate an estate. The lawyer may charge an hourly fee, a flat fee, a percentage fee based upon the size of the estate, or some combination of all of the above. In addition, there will be assorted court costs and related fees. Note that your family is under no obligation to hire the attorney who drafted your will just because the attorney keeps the original document in his vault.

It's difficult to give a precise figure for the cost of probate. It varies based on the size of the estate and how long the process takes, which in some cases can be years. It also varies greatly from state to state. In some states, there are statutes regulating attorney fees in probate proceedings. An often-mentioned rule-of-thumb figure is that the probate process will deplete two to ten percent of the value of the estate. If the estate is contested, then the cost is anyone's guess.

Except for the smallest of estates, this almost certainly will be considerably more than you would have paid an estate-planning attorney to design an estate plan that could have by-passed the probate process. So if your failure to plan is driven by thriftiness, it's likely you're being penny-wise and pound-foolish. And, of course, the dollar cost doesn't reflect the time, inconvenience, anguish, and humiliation that the probate process can cause the family.

Adding to the potential cost of death, a probate estate must be opened in *every* state where you own real estate. For example, if a New York resident dies owning a condominium in Florida, the executor must hire a separate attorney in Florida to open up an ancillary probate estate, because New York courts have no jurisdiction over the Florida property.

Passing your assets to your heirs through the probate process is often the least convenient, most expensive option available. Yet probate is the option that many people unintentionally choose for their family, simply by failing to take the necessary steps to avoid it. A will alone will not avoid probate.

Probate fees

California's probate fees, including attorney's and executor's fees, are based on gross estate assets before any reduction for debts (for example, the total value of your house, rather than your equity in it). The fees, which are probably about average for the fifty states, are set by statute, though the attorney and executor may charge less. These fees do not include filing costs and bond premiums; nor do they include appraisal and other special fees that may be involved in the sale of assets, or the fees charged for tax preparation, which would be paid regardless of whether there is probate. Additionally, if there are other complicating factors, such as a will challenge, the court may approve higher attorney and executor fees.

Value of Estate	Rate
Up to $100,000	4%
Next $100,000	3%
Next $800,000	2%
Next $9 million	1%
Next $15 million	0.5%
Over $25 million	A reasonable fee to be determined by the court.
Source: California probate code	

If the executor and attorney *each* receive the statutory fee, you can double the amount noted above. In many states, attorneys and executors are simply entitled to "reasonable compensation." If it takes years to close an estate, the attorneys can take a huge slice—and given this fact, they don't always seem to be in a hurry.

The Advantages of Probate

Although I generally advocate the use of revocable living trusts to avoid probate (discussed in the next chapter), sometimes administering an estate via probate is better than avoiding it. Some reasons that probate can be an advantage:

- Creditors' claims can be cut off more quickly using a probate proceeding than if assets are passed through a trust. Claims on a probate estate must be made within a certain time period—usually six to twelve months, depending on the state—provided proper notice of death is given. After that period of time, all creditor claims are cut off. In contrast, creditors' claims against a trust are treated like claims against the deceased as an individual. Often, this means that claims can be pressed well beyond a six-to-twelve-month time frame. When there are potential creditors, some people choose to negate this problem through a simple probate conducted on nominal assets. It works like this: The vast majority of the estate is in the trust, but some small amount, say $10, is put through probate for the sole purpose of eliminating claims on the entire estate once the probate period ends. Even though only a small amount of money passed through probate, this may eliminate claims on the entire estate, provided proper notification is made to creditors.

- You trust your trustees only to a certain extent. If one of them is a closet embezzler, the trust could get wiped out before anyone has a chance to discover what's been done. While this book supports the privacy afforded by funded revocable living trusts, it must be acknowledged that sometimes there is an advantage in having the probate court keep an eye on things. Selecting a bank trustee (also discussed in the next chapter) may ease your mind with regard to the possibility of a trustee looting or otherwise completely botching a trust.

- With a probate estate you have the choice of either a calendar or fiscal year income-tax-year election. With a trust, if there is no associated probate, the calendar year must be used. Why is this a problem? For ninety-nine people out of one hundred it isn't, but some people like to use a fiscal year election to delay their filing deadline.

REAL LIFE STORIES

My own estate plan is a good example of an intentional probate: My profession, estate-planning law, is one where there is
theoretically no end to the threat of liability. If the heirs of one of
my clients decide to try to sue me even after my death, perhaps
thinking that I'd made some costly mistake in their parents' estate plan, they might be able to move forward with a case.
That's why I've arranged to have a pro forma probate proceeding done on minimal assets after my death, even though substantially all of my assets are held in trust. Anything is possible,
and I sleep better knowing that some lawsuit won't pop up and
devastate my heirs after I'm gone and unable to defend myself.

Simplified Probate—Independent Administration

Many states have reformed their probate codes to allow a
simplified probate known as independent administration. This
allows a will to be probated with virtually no supervision from
the probate court, and it can significantly lower probate costs.

If all of the creditors and beneficiaries go along with this simplified process, the probate can be accomplished with as few as
two court appearances, one opening the estate and one closing it.
In between, the executor can collect, inventory, and administer
the estate and pay debts without constantly checking in with the
probate judge.

But if a creditor or beneficiary becomes disenchanted with
the executor, that party may object to the independent administration and the estate may be put into a full-blown probate.

Loss of Privacy in Probate

Probate is a public process. Anyone can examine your probate court file, including your will, if you have one, because it must be filed as a public document. In addition, a notice of your death must be filed in a local newspaper so that any creditors unknown to the executor can initiate claims. (In the absence of probate, there is no requirement to publish a notice, although if there is a will, that must still be filed in the court. However, if the will is a "pour-over will"—discussed in chapter 9—the information that can be gleaned from it is minimal.) In probate, all of your assets are inventoried in the court file. Anyone can attend the probate hearings and examine the court files, as they are open to the general public. If this doesn't bother you, perhaps it should: Do you want just anyone to have access to information about your beneficiaries, including their addresses and the amounts of their bequests?

Probate without a Will

When a person dies intestate, that is, without a will, probate costs can be particularly high. For example, in Cook County, Illinois (Chicago and suburbs), in addition to the attorney's fees, the usual court fee of $220, and $120 to publish a mandated notice to potential creditors, a surety bond must be posted to guarantee that the estate is handled correctly.

For a $1 million estate, that bond would add another yearly fee of $2,760 to the cost of your probate for as long as the estate is open; the larger the estate, the higher the bond cost. Attorney's fees, always a consideration, generally run higher with intestate estates than when there is an uncontested will, because the attorney might have to:

- spend more time with the decedent's family determining the proper heirs

- spend more time in front of the court proving who the rightful heirs are under the law

---

HOW TO DEFEAT PROCRASTINATION

Get help from someone. There is no rule you must do everything yourself.

Beyond the probate fees incurred in an intestate estate, dying without a will creates a few other problems.

The probate court determines who gets your assets, when, and in what percentages, according to the preset laws of intestacy, which vary from state to state. The intestate distribution system is designed to be fair, and it might work for your family, but often things don't work out exactly as you would expect.

The probate court will also determine which person shall act as guardian for any minor children, and who should be your personal representative, collecting your assets, paying your debts, and distributing your remaining assets. If your children are minors, guardianship will have to be established in a separate probate proceeding and a surety bond will have to be paid every year until they reach the age of majority, usually 18 or 21. At that time, they will get their entire remaining inheritance, all at once, with no strings attached—party time!

REAL-LIFE STORIES

Gerald, 45, found out the hard way how the laws of intestacy can be inappropriate. When his father died without a will (Gerald's mother had passed away years before), the estate was divided evenly between Gerald and his brother, David. Sounds

REAL-LIFE STORIES

fair, right? Under normal circumstances, it would have been. But David has severe disabilities that leave him eligible for government assistance when all his assets have been depleted. Thus, David's inheritance meant that he received less government assistance until the inheritance was completely used up. It was as if the government had inherited the money! Since Gerald provides his brother with everything that government programs do not, his father should have thought ahead and left David's money in a supplemental needs trust with Gerald as trustee.

Probate with a Will

If you have a will when you die, your assets will go, eventually, to the people or charities that you name in your will. Writing a will also means that you get to nominate the guardian for your minor children. You also select the executor along with the trustee for any testamentary trusts, which are trusts that become effective at your death (as opposed to living trusts which go into effect during your lifetime).

Other ways a will can simplify the process:

- a will can provide for a waiver of bond for the executor of your will, which will cut out part of the probate cost
- a will can provide for independent administration by the executor as opposed to court-supervised administration, keeping court appearances to a minimum

Selecting an Executor

The skills needed to be the executor of a will are similar to those required to be a trustee of your trust. Very often, the person selected to be trustee is named executor.

A major difference between the two roles is the potential duration of the time commitment. The trustee role can last for a long period of time, since the job might go on for years, especially where minor children are involved. Hopefully, probate will not last for years, although under a nasty set of circumstances, it can.

Even with a will, your executor will have to go to the county probate court and obtain a court order (usually called letters of office or letters testamentary) to get control of your assets. A will, on its own, does not confer this authority. It simply tells the probate court where and how your assets should be distributed upon your death.

The probate court establishes a will's authenticity and officially appoints the executor named in the will. Having a will does simplify the probate proceeding because the court does not have to make choices for you. However, it does not eliminate the need for probate. Meanwhile, your assets are in probate and it may be difficult for your heirs to gain access to them, a potential problem if your loved ones are depending on these funds.

REAL-LIFE STORIES

Tim and Diane died together in an automobile accident four years ago, leaving three children, ages 16, 12, and 11. They had done no estate planning, so their estate went into probate. The couple's estate was worth over $1 million—at least until probate. Guardianship proceedings can be particularly expen-

REAL-LIFE STORIES

sive and Tim's and Diane's families each argued that they should receive custody of the children. By the time the probate was over, more than $50,000 had been drained, and the children had spent half a year in limbo, uncertain where they would be living.

A year later, Tim and Diane's oldest child, Jon, reached age 18 and inherited his share of their money. Without trusts, all the money went into his hands on his birthday with no controls in place. Unfortunately, since the probate is a public process, an unscrupulous "salesman" knew the details of the inheritance, and convinced Jon to put the lion's share of his money into a series of terrible investments. Jon was not left with enough to pay his college tuition.

Transferring Property upon Death without Probate

If a will isn't enough to avoid probate, what is? A number of different mechanisms can enable your beneficiary to take over your assets upon your death without probate. Some work better than others, depending on your situation.

1. Designating a beneficiary

Certain assets such as life insurance policies, annuities, and various retirement accounts, including IRAs and 401(k)s, typically allow you to designate a beneficiary to receive payment upon your death.

Banks, brokerages, and many mutual funds allow similar automatic transfers to a beneficiary upon your death. Such accounts may be called POD (Payable on

Death) or TOD (Transfer on Death) accounts, and they allow such assets to be transferred without probate. This strategy is not available for all assets, however; most notably, it isn't an option for real estate. Moreover, it might fail if you don't name a beneficiary, or if your beneficiary dies before (or with) you and you failed to name a contingent beneficiary.

2. Joint tenancy with rights of survivorship

You can name one or more persons as joint tenants of certain assets. A surviving joint tenant on the account will have access to the account after your death (and during your life—the person you select as a joint tenant thereafter has the same right to the account as you do; he could, for example, unilaterally withdraw all the money at *any* time).

It might be more accurate to say that joint tenancy postpones probate, rather than avoids it. When the surviving joint tenant dies, the asset must then go through probate, unless the survivor has retitled the asset or added a new joint tenant. We'll cover various pluses and minuses of joint tenancy later in this chapter.

3. Assets held in trust

A revocable self-declaration of trust is a simple and versatile way to transfer assets upon death. You fund the trust by transferring the ownership of assets into the trust during your lifetime. From that point, you no longer own the assets as an individual; you own them as the trustee of your trust.

Upon your death, the assets in the trust will be distributed according to the provisions of your trust agreement. See chapter 8 for more about trusts.

4. Small estates

Small estates often can be transferred with an easy affidavit or some other simplified procedure to shortcut probate, as long as there are no unpaid creditors or disputes among the potential heirs. States vary in their

definitions of a "small estate," but usually real estate
cannot be dealt with via an affidavit. See State Survey #2.

5. Buy-sell agreements

A buy-sell agreement may be used to transfer a pri-
vately owned business such as a corporation or a partnership. In one typical structure, a life-insurance policy is
purchased by the partnership for each partner. When one
partner dies, the proceeds of the policy are used to buy
out the interests of the deceased partner by paying an appropriate amount directly to his family, without probate.
See chapter 12 for more details.

6. Personal property

Modest items of tangible personal property, such as
clothing, furniture, and jewelry, *usually* can be divided
among family members, without acrimony and without
probate. Of course, sometimes the biggest family battles
are over items with little market value but enormous sentimental value. Most estate plans deal with personal property in a cursory manner because listing all your "stuff"
and deciding who gets what would be a time-consuming
task—and you expect, or at least hope, that your beneficiaries will be fair in dealing with each other. However, if
you fear a family battle over tangible personal property,
then take a look at some of my suggestions in chapter 12
about how to resolve a potentially difficult situation.

7. Land trusts

Some states, notably Illinois, Arizona, and Florida,
allow a bank or trust company to nominally own real estate in the form of a land trust. Under this arrangement,
the true owner's name is hidden from the public record
and is named only in the bank/trust company's internal
records as a beneficiary.

This beneficial owner typically retains the power of
direction to transfer the property and designates contingent beneficiaries who become the new beneficial owners

upon his death. You have to pay the bank or trust company to establish and terminate a land trust, along with annual fees.

Contrary to what many people believe, land trusts do not protect the beneficial owner from liability arising out of accidents occurring on the subject property, nor do they allow the property to escape the reach of the beneficial owner's creditors, but they do avoid probate.

LOOKING OUT FOR FIDO

In most states, an animal cannot be the beneficiary of a will or trust. However, people often provide for their pets by making arrangements for their care and leaving money for the person providing that care, preferably in the form of a "salary" for the duration of the arrangement.

There are also a number of companies that provide pet care after an owner's death. One advertises warm meals and heated beds (rather than cages), private rooms, daily walks along the pond, ball throwing games, swimming, and a lot of soothing petting and personal interaction. Massage therapy is also an option.

Joint Tenancy with Rights of Survivorship: Not Always the Answer

Joint tenancy with rights of survivorship is a very popular way for two or more people to own an undivided interest in an asset. In some ways, joint tenancy's appeal is understandable: Upon the death of one joint tenant, the other joint tenant (or tenants) automatically gains control of the entire asset.

Little if any paperwork is needed to handle the transfer of

ownership. No question, it's easy to set up. Unfortunately, there may be potential problems, particularly when joint tenancy is used between two people who are not husband and wife, or when it's the exclusive planning device for a husband and wife who would derive much greater benefits from a more thorough estate-planning process.

Joint Tenancy versus Tenancy in Common

Tenancy in common is not the same as joint tenancy, although the two terms are sometimes confused. Under joint tenancy, ownership is passed upon the death of one tenant to the other tenant or tenants. Under tenancy in common, ownership is transferred *not* to the surviving tenant or tenants, but to whomever the deceased tenant directs. Alternatively, ownership may go to the deceased's estate. The asset remains divided among the surviving original tenant and the new tenant(s) in common.

For example, suppose you own an apartment building in joint tenancy with your brother. When you die, the asset becomes his. But if you and your brother own the building through a tenancy in common, when you die, your brother still owns only his half, while your half is transferred to your estate, or to whomever you designate in your will or trust.

Spousal Joint Tenancy

One of the most common uses of joint tenancy is between husband and wife. Couples often settle on joint tenancy of assets as a convenient way to avoid probate. Possessions held in joint tenancy do in fact avoid probate initially. But a close look illustrates some potential problems.

For example, consider a couple who owns their house in this

manner. When the first spouse dies, the house will pass to the second without probate, as the couple had intended. Unless additional estate planning is done, however, the house will face probate when the second spouse dies. And if both spouses die at more or less the same time, probate will be required.

Meanwhile, assets held in joint tenancy between spouses are not fully shielded from estate taxes. True, upon the first death the assets pass to the surviving spouse without estate taxes taking a share, but what happens when the surviving spouse dies? The entire estate might face estate taxes. We'll cover this topic in more detail in chapter 10.

More important, joint tenancy can lead to estates being divided in ways that would not have met with the deceased's wishes. For example, if a widower with two children remarries and puts his property in joint tenancy with his new wife, his children will not inherit any of the joint tenancy assets when he dies—they go completely to the new wife.

This is not to say that spousal joint tenancy never makes sense. It's a perfectly viable option when used properly, but only when its limitations are understood and various consequences have been considered.

Nonspousal Joint Tenancy

Joint tenancy between spouses might have a few complications, but larger problems develop when people attempt to use joint tenancy between nonspouses. Often, such arrangements are made between a parent and adult child. Even if disasters such as those discussed below don't occur, joint tenancy can complicate the joint tenants' lives. To sell real estate held in joint tenancy, for example, all joint tenants must sign the deed or other necessary paperwork. At worst, this can be a nightmare if the joint tenants do not agree on specifics, or at least inconvenient if one cannot be reached.

While joint tenancy financial assets, such as bank accounts, can be set up on an either/or basis, so that only one signature is required for transactions, this usually cannot be done with real estate. If one of the joint tenants becomes incompetent, either a guardianship or a durable power of attorney for property would be required to transfer the asset.

Let's examine what can happen after Dad dies and Mom puts the house in joint tenancy with her son, in the hope that it will pass to him after her death without probate. Such an arrangement can lead to potential disasters:

- if the son files for bankruptcy, is involved in a divorce proceeding, or is otherwise sued, the house could be lost, even though the son had nothing to do with its purchase, and does not live in the house
- mother and son might become estranged. With joint tenancy, he would have as much right to decide how the house is used as she does.
- the son could predecease his mother, throwing her estate into probate when she dies
- when the son becomes outright owner of the house after his mother's death, he need not respect her intentions. Perhaps she has three children, and meant for the proceeds from the sale of the house to be shared equally. If the son who was named joint tenant decides he'd rather take the whole thing for himself, his siblings might have no legal recourse.
- if the son is married and he and his wife are living in the house, the daughter-in-law's signature might be required for sale because she has marital rights. But what if the marriage is on the rocks and the wife refuses to cooperate?
- tax consequences must be carefully analyzed. Gift-tax returns must be (but often aren't) filed, and a carryover basis can lead to income taxes upon an eventual sale. Tax issues are discussed below.

Tax Consequences of Nonspousal Joint Tenancy

Another potential problem with the use of intergenerational joint tenancies—either parent and child, or grandparent and grandchild—are the various tax consequences.

Income Tax Consequences

To understand the income tax implications of joint tenancies, it's necessary to understand the way the government taxes capital gains. When an asset increases in value between the time it is purchased and the time it is sold, capital gains taxes generally must be paid on the profit.

This is true whether the asset in question is a share of stock, a house, a piece of art, or just about anything else, although real estate does receive favorable tax treatment under certain circumstances. Just take the sale price, subtract the cost basis—that is, the initial cost of the asset plus money invested in it since, such as home improvement costs in the case of real estate—and you have the amount subject to the capital gains tax.

For highly appreciated assets, such as real estate or stocks owned for long periods of time, this tax can represent a substantial portion of the total value of the asset.

Fortunately, at this time the government provides a measure of relief from these taxes when an item is passed at death. When an appreciated asset is transferred by reason of its owner's death, the cost basis of the asset is stepped up to its value at the former owner's date of death. Upon subsequent sale by the new owner, income tax is paid only on the appreciation following the date of death. Any appreciation during the previous owner's lifetime escapes income tax.

Let's take a simplified example: Assume your parents bought

shares of a certain stock for $10,000 decades ago. You inherited the stock upon the death of a parent two years ago, when it was worth $250,000. This year you decided to sell it, when the total value was at $275,000. You don't have to pay capital gains taxes on the $240,000 profit over your parents' purchase price, just on the final $25,000 increase in value.

That can be a pretty hefty tax advantage. But it applies only when assets are transferred at death. If an asset were gifted during the donor's lifetime, there would be no step-up in cost basis. Upon a subsequent sale of the asset by the person who received the gift, whether before or after the death of the original donor, capital gains taxes then would be required on the entire appreciation from the time of the original purchase.

How does this affect joint tenants? In part, it depends on the type of asset. For bank and brokerage accounts, the formation of a joint tenancy is not an immediate gift, unless a noncontributing joint tenant withdraws assets. Assets so withdrawn receive no step-up upon the death of the contributor. As to other assets, such as a house, the formation of the joint tenancy may be an immediate gift and lose a half step up, depending upon IRS treatment. Usually, if the surviving joint tenant made no contribution to the asset, then the asset is 100 percent includible in the contributing joint tenant's estate, and there would be a full step-up. However, there may be circumstances where the IRS would deny such a step-up, leading to potential capital gains taxes.

Often a child's name is put on an asset as joint tenant for convenience purposes only and the facts will dictate whether a gift has in fact been made. Paradoxically, the filing of a federal gift-tax return may result in negative implications regarding future step-ups. However, if the gift tax return is required and no filing is made, penalties can be assessed. The IRS can go either way on these types of "transfers" depending on various factors, including the type of asset, whether proper filings are made, local law, and even including which agent is doing the audit.

Step-up Loophole Closed

Perhaps you've noticed that the step-up rules appear to open an even greater tax-saving loophole: If you have a family member likely to die soon, it could make sense to transfer highly appreciated assets to this person. Then have that family member leave the asset to you, thereby getting the advantages of the step-up without going through the trouble of dying.

The government has closed this loophole by adding an exception to the step-up rules: If appreciated property is transferred to a donee who dies within one year of the transfer, and the donor or the donor's spouse indirectly benefits, the step-up is negated.

New Law

Chapter 10 contains a discussion about the elimination of estate taxes. What the government gives with one hand, it can take away with the other. The step-up for assets transferred by means of a person's death will be abolished for people dying after December 31, 2009, as part of the Tax Relief Act of 2001, whereby estate taxes are repealed for people dying in 2010.

At that time, with certain exceptions, capital gains taxes are scheduled to replace estate taxes as a revenue generator. So save all records regarding purchase price and any adjustments because your heirs might need them to determine the capital gains tax on your assets sold after your death.

Estate Tax Considerations

As mentioned above, estate tax strategies are covered in some depth in chapters 10, 11, and 12, but for now take a quick look at more negative results using joint tenancies. Assets held in joint tenancy might avoid probate, but contrary to popular belief, just because an asset passes outside your probate estate, it doesn't mean it won't be included in your taxable estate.

The general rule is that the entire value of a joint tenancy asset is included in the taxable estate of the first joint tenant to die, except to the extent that the surviving joint tenant can prove a contribution toward the purchase of the asset. If nonspousal joint tenants sell and reinvest joint tenancy assets, proving contribution by one joint tenant or another becomes exceedingly complex and can be subject to scrutiny by the IRS, which is not known to be sympathetic to the difficulties inherent in the process.

A potential nightmare of nonspousal joint tenancies is double taxation, which delights the IRS. A joint tenancy asset can be taxed in the estate of the first joint tenant to die to the extent that the surviving joint tenant cannot prove contribution—and then it can be taxed again in the surviving tenant's estate.

So when is nonspousal joint tenancy between a parent and child appropriate? Generally only when all of the following are true:

- there is only one surviving or competent parent, and only one child
- the child is unmarried
- the child is an adult and can be trusted implicitly
- the parent has more than enough assets even without the assets in the joint tenancy
- the parent is relatively elderly—that is, likely to be within a few years of death

Tenancy by the Entirety

Some states provide for a form of ownership called tenancy by the entirety (T/E). A T/E is similar to a joint tenancy in that upon the death of one of the tenants the asset held in T/E automatically passes to the survivor. The major difference is that a tenancy by the entirety may be created only by a married couple, and may be severed only by agreement of both spouses. Also, in most states a T/E generally can be used only for the couple's principal residence, not other assets or properties. Its major advantage over a joint tenancy is that it shields the principal residence from creditors who have a claim against just one spouse (the asset is not protected if the liability is a joint one).

Tenancy by the entirety can be a useful asset protection tool when one or both spouses are employed in professions susceptible to lawsuits. Upon the death of the surviving owner, however, property owned as tenancy by the entirety does need to be probated, and if the surviving tenant has liabilities, the creditors could then get to the asset.

As we saw in this chapter, there are numerous ways to avoid probate, including the use of trusts (discussed more fully in the next chapter). Some of the shortcut methods, such as joint tenancies, may be simple and inexpensive to set up—yet do only half the job. Will money saved now result in an estate drain upon your death?

Action Plan Seven: Don't Stop Now!

Keep your family out of court:

1. *Today*, review the way your assets are owned. Consider whether they will avoid probate upon your death (and if you are married, if they will avoid probate upon the death of the surviving spouse).

2. If your assets are held in joint tenancy as a convenience only, consider that that convenience can be outweighed by horrendous results. A typical situation that has people "spinning in their graves": If your house is put into joint tenancy with your second spouse, upon your death she will not be legally obligated to share that asset with your children from

Action Plan Seven: Don't Stop Now!

your first marriage. Moral obligations often mean very little in a court of law.

3. Compare the potential financial costs of probate with the amount that a complete estate plan, including a trust, will cost you.

4. Consider the loss of privacy in a probate proceeding. Would it bother you that anyone interested in looking at your probate can see an inventory of your assets along with the names and addresses of your beneficiaries?

CHAPTER 8

Revocable Living Trusts

"Put not your trust in money, but put your money in trust."
—Oliver Wendell Holmes, Jr.

In common law, a trust is defined simply as a right of property, real or personal, held by one party for the benefit of another. Trusts can be created for any purpose (so long as that purpose is not illegal or against public policy) and can be changed by the creator at any time.

You can avoid probate with a fully funded revocable trust. To establish a trust, you need:

- a beneficiary
- a trustee who has fiduciary responsibilities toward the beneficiary with respect to the property—someone willing to look after the beneficiary's interests when it comes to the assets, and be held to a high standard in doing so, and
- property identified as belonging to the trust and actually delivered to the trust

Revocable living trusts are also known as living trusts or inter vivos trusts (Latin for "between living persons"). By any name, a revocable trust is distinct from other forms of trusts in that the trust may be amended or revoked during your lifetime.

When people think of trusts, they often think of banks. Many banks have trust departments that can act as trustee for all types of trusts. However, you can create a "self-declaration of trust," where you, the grantor, act as your own trustee or cotrustee. You name the successor trustee to act on your behalf should you become incapacitated or die. Unless you choose to avail yourself of the expertise offered by a professional trustee, no bank need be involved with your trust in any way.

Four words describe a revocable self-declaration of trust—*You control it completely!*

A revocable self-declaration of trust can be a very useful estate-planning tool—the centerpiece of many estate plans. You no longer own your assets directly; rather, you own and control them as trustee of your trust.

This might seem like mere semantics—and in some ways it is—but it has a number of advantages. For example, should you become incapacitated, your trust is still as healthy as ever. And, properly constructed, it can operate in your absence. The successor trustee you have named in the trust simply takes over the job of managing the assets in the trust, according to whatever rules or guidelines you've laid out. As a result, the courts do not need to intervene through a probate proceeding, and there's no point at which the assets are out of your control or the control of your designated trustee.

Mechanics of a Revocable Living Trust

In order for a revocable trust to be an efficient way to avoid probate, it must be funded with your assets. Funding a self-declaration of trust with your assets means transferring the assets from your name as an individual or joint tenant to your name as trustee of your revocable trust.

After the creation of the trust, you should take title to newly acquired assets as trustee as well. Except to the extent that other, perhaps more sophisticated estate tax or creditor protection strategies dictate otherwise, all real estate, no matter where it is located, should be transferred into the trust, avoiding multiple "ancillary" probates in every state where you own real estate.

HOW TO DEFEAT PROCRASTINATION

Make deadlines and mark them in your calendar. If you walk out of your attorney's office and do not do the follow-up work of funding your trust, much of your planning has been wasted, so set yourself a deadline, mark your calendar accordingly and, if necessary, get help.

Because you control your trust completely, you continue to control the assets owned by the trust. If you want to sell an asset and buy another one, you simply do it. The only difference is that instead of transacting business as an individual or joint tenant, you now do so as a trustee.

So what will change? Not much. You may be required to add the word "trustee" to your signature, but most financial institutions won't require that. There is no additional bookkeeping required. Income, gains, and losses flow through to you as an individual or married couple, and the figures plug right into your regular 1040 tax form the same as they did before you established your trust. If you file a joint return, you can continue to do so. No special tax ID number is required during your lifetime—you can continue to use your social security number on all of your accounts.

There are no ongoing fees associated with maintaining a self-declaration of trust. Unless you later need to amend the trust, the cost of the revocable living trust is a relatively modest onetime expense. Upon your death, your next-named successor trustee has immediate control over your assets according to your written directions, without any involvement by the probate court.

Benefits of a Fully Funded Revocable Living Trust

A fully funded revocable living trust often serves as the centerpiece of a complete estate plan. It accomplishes the essential purposes of a will—to give your assets to your beneficiaries—smoothly, without probate.

You do not give up any control of the assets in the trust while living. A revocable living trust will provide for a successor trustee to begin acting immediately upon your death or during any period of incompetence. When you do die, your assets will be distributed per your instructions, or continue to be held in trust—whatever you direct in the trust document.

The reason the process works so smoothly is simple: The trust owns the assets, and a trust does not die or become incompetent. It continues under a new set of circumstances already anticipated in the trust instrument, with different people in control for the benefit of new beneficiaries. The trust can continue during your surviving spouse's lifetime, during the lifetime of your children, and possibly during the lifetime of your grandchildren—even if they are not yet born at the time of your death.

If your revocable living trust is fully funded with your assets, there will be no probate when you die. Your successor trustee or heirs might choose to consult with a lawyer to understand your trust, but even so, the legal fees involved in the process should be reduced dramatically, since no assets have to pass through probate and, thus, no lawyers will have to go to court.

Funding Your Trust

Some initial paperwork will be required to transfer assets to the trust or change beneficiary designations of your assets. This is known as funding the trust, and can be compared to preprobating your own estate without using a court. You can have your attorney handle the funding from start to finish, or lower your legal fees by having him simply provide you with sample letters and guidelines to assist you with making the changes on your own.

By avoiding probate, a revocable living trust is more difficult to contest than a will. Any person who has standing to make a claim in court, such as a potential beneficiary or creditor, can contest a will. The probate court might disregard a will if convinced that the will is defective.

A revocable living trust "attacker" must initiate the battle by filing a probate court action. Without the trust, a probate estate would already be open. Legally, filing a probate court action and attacking a trust may be a more difficult maneuver than simply contesting a will in an existing probate proceeding.

Examples: With and without a Revocable Living Trust

What will happen to your estate if you have a fully funded revocable living trust? What if you never get around to it? The answers to these questions depend on your personal situation. If you have a relatively small estate, the effect of failing to implement a revocable living trust might be little more than a few time-consuming tasks for your family. But if you have a large estate, your procrastination might lead to hefty probate-related fees, or cost you opportunities for estate-tax savings, a topic we'll cover in more depth in chapter 10.

Here's a look at a few examples:

Example 1

No spouse, no will, no living trust: You may have created significant problems for those you've left behind.

- The probate process begins.
- The court appoints an administrator who may or may not be the person you would have selected.
- After your heirs post a surety bond, likely costing them hundreds or even thousands of dollars yearly, the court supervises the payment of all your debts.
- Various court costs and legal fees will be paid, draining 2 to 10 percent of the value of your estate, perhaps much more.
- After a minimum of six months, distribution of your remaining assets is made according to a preset formula of intestate succession, making no distinction between specific needs of your heirs and not taking your intentions into account.
- Until probate is finished, it may be difficult for your heirs to make transactions related to your accounts.
- Meanwhile, anyone who wishes to take a look at the estate may do so simply by requesting the probate court file.

Example 2

No spouse and no living trust, but you leave a will: The executor will be someone you selected, and the assets will go to the persons or charities you picked, in the percentages or amounts stated in your will.

- Assuming no one disputes your will, and you waived the surety bond requirement, and permit independent administration in the will, probate fees will be kept to a minimum.

- If there are no special circumstances, such as beneficiaries disputing your wishes, it shouldn't be a total disaster.
- However, your will is open to public examination, and it will be at least six months before your heirs fully inherit.

Example 3

No spouse—but your assets are owned by a revocable living trust: At your death, the successor trustee can immediately and without court order direct the bank and broker to act in whatever terms you've laid out in the trust.

- There are no court costs or court-related attorney fees.
- The assets are never in a probate "twilight zone."
- There is no public record. It's that simple.

Selecting a Trustee: Banks versus Individuals

If you're acting as your own trustee with a self-declaration of trust, you can name either an individual or a corporate trustee, such as a bank's trust department, as successor trustee. Of course, you don't want to name anyone or any institution as a possible trustee if you don't trust the individual's or institution's ethics or judgment.

After you select one or more individuals as successor trustee (after yourself), you may also select one or more backups, in case your original choice or choices cannot act (e.g., if they die before you, or with you, or become incapacitated).

You can select individual cotrustees who would work together, but be careful about using more than two or three; above that, your cotrustee structure might create gridlock. While you are living and competent, you can change your choice of trustee at any time, just as you can change any of the trust's other terms.

Some attorneys suggest to their clients that *they* be named as successor trustee. Whether this is appropriate or not may depend on the type of relationship you have with the lawyer. A longtime family lawyer who is intimate with your family's dynamics may make a great trustee or cotrustee, but if your relationship is just beginning, she may not be the best choice.

If you decide that a professional trustee is the best choice, consider the resources available to the trustee. In my opinion, banks are usually better suited than law firms when it comes to investing trust assets and distributing money to heirs.

It's also reasonable to give your beneficiaries the authority to select or remove the bank, so that control isn't completely handed over. If the bank is "untouchable," it may act arrogantly toward your beneficiaries, whereas if it can be removed, it may be more responsive.

When selecting an individual trustee (and the same reasoning applies when selecting an agent for property or executor), you should be looking for two qualities:

- First, you obviously want someone who is trustworthy— who won't steal the money from the beneficiaries.
- Second, you want someone who is going to live up to the responsibility—not put the bank and brokerage statements in a drawer and forget about them.

If you're concerned that an individual you wish to select as trustee might be overwhelmed by the complexity of the trust— an argument that bank trust departments often use to encourage the use of their services—simply grant him or her the authority to appoint a cotrustee, such as a bank, an attorney, or a CPA for help in managing the trust.

Another argument banks make is that emotional family issues sometimes require the detachment of an independent trustee. For example, if you're concerned your children might not get along with each other when it comes to handling your estate, a bank might be the most appropriate trustee. Perhaps naming one child as trustee might offend another, especially if that would leave one child in charge of distributing money to siblings.

I often suggest that adult children be made the trustee over their own trust share once the trust divides. This minimizes the potential conflict between siblings, but does not address the problem of one or more children with a history of making poor financial judgments.

Banks can be coldhearted institutions, but they don't get sick, die, or move away; they don't share old family grudges or rivalries; and they will understand the documents. For all of these reasons, banks are often a good choice as trustee.

Their drawback is cost. A typical yearly bank fee is likely to be in the neighborhood of one to two percent. That might not sound like much, but over time it can add up. Of course, the net cost of not using a professional trustee could be much higher than a bank fee if the individuals you select do a poor job. As intelligent as your trustee may be, your estate might well be more money than that person has handled before, and it can be a daunting task.

Still, the fees charged by banks often make them inappropriate for small trust estates.

- As a rule of thumb, unless your estate is worth more than $250,000, the costs may be prohibitive. Some banks have minimum trust account sizes that might be higher than that.
- If the value of your trust is under $1 million and you prefer to use a bank as trustee, it might make sense to consider a local, suburban bank rather than a downtown behemoth, where costs and minimum account sizes generally are higher, and the amount of attention paid to small trusts may be less.

Liability issues also should be considered. If an individual dissipates trust assets, he may be legally liable to your beneficiaries, but it does them no good if he hasn't got the money to pay them. On the other hand, if a bank ruins a trust, your heirs would have a better chance to recover the assets in a lawsuit.

Investment Policy Statement

For clear communications and as protection from liability, it is useful for a trustee to state, in writing, an investment policy.

Such a document can articulate objectives such as investment guidelines, risk tolerance, performance goals, diversification requirements, communication expectations, and review parameters. Having a written statement is especially useful when the trust's performance is inadequate compared to the overall market, because it may be used to explain the trustee's actions to a disgruntled beneficiary. A financial planner or your attorney can help you draft an investment policy statement.

Action Plan Eight: You're Making Progress!

A three-step plan for creating and maintaining your trust:

1. Decide whom you would like to have as a trustee. Is one of your children particularly responsible or good with money? If none of them would make an appropriate choice, what about a sibling or lifelong friend? Consider whether selecting one of your children over another would cause hurt feelings.

2. Would a professional trustee such as a bank be more suitable, for example, if your estate is large or complex? If so, call this week for a meeting with your bank's trust representative and discuss how the bank would handle your trust.

Action Plan Eight: You're Making Progress!

3. If you have a trust, make sure it is funded correctly. If you have not followed the steps required to fund your trust, begin the process this week. Gather your bank, brokerage, mutual fund, and other statements and start doing the appropriate paperwork. If you need help, call your attorney or financial adviser. Put a deadline in your calendar for one month from today to complete any restructuring required.

CHAPTER 9

Deciding Who Gets
What and How

"When you have to make a choice and don't make it,
that in itself is a choice."

—William James

Proceeding with a revocable living trust means making some decisions about who gets your assets when you die. The trust can divide your estate and direct payment to your beneficiaries according to almost any legitimate formula creative minds can devise.

Many people without a surviving spouse provide that upon death their assets are split into equal shares and immediately distributed to their grown children. If the children are not competent adults, restrictions can be added on how the assets benefit them, and additional provisions can pass benefits on to grandchildren.

Others, either because they have no children, have children with differing levels of need, have poor relationships with certain children, or have very close friends or other relatives they wish to consider, devise their own formulas. Some states require that a certain percentage of your assets be given to a surviving spouse, but in most states there is absolutely no law demanding you include or exclude any individual.

You simply need to explain the details in your will or trust. If you leave someone out, you might consider briefly explaining your thinking as well, so there's no confusion or hurt feelings, but this is certainly not required. Language such as "for reasons best known to my son Bob, he gets nothing" can certainly suffice.

THINK

When favoring one child over another in some manner, either by giving one child more assets than the other or by giving one child more authority than the other, take some time to consider the effect this may have on future family relations. Sibling rivalry has been around as long as Cain versus Abel. Do you want to fan the flames of sibling rivalry, keeping it alive into the next generation?

Limiting the Use of Your Money

One way to protect your assets while giving control to your children is to make each of your adult children trustee of his or her own share of the estate, keeping the assets in trust instead of turning them over outright. You can impose further restrictions by making the principal off-limits, giving your children access only to the income generated by the trust and perhaps additional distributions for select purposes, such as health care, education, emergencies, or to buy a house.

Such provisions are not overly restrictive but provide some protection from outside influences. Because the child/trustee does not own the assets outright, the assets *may* be shielded from your child's creditors, particularly the child's spouse, if handled correctly, and may also be excluded from the child's estate at death. Language such as this may allow for generation skipping (discussed in chapter 12), in effect making the gift to your grandchildren while still giving your children access to the money during their lifetimes in such a way that the gift is not includable in their own estate. However, to strengthen those aspects of the trust that protect it from outside influences, it may be better to name a trustee other than the child to handle her share.

Some other options:

- You can tie access to the money in the trust to age, so that your children gain some access at 18, perhaps, but don't receive full access until age 25 (I have seen restrictions placed upon a child until she reaches age 70). You can extend such provisions to include the ages at which your grandchildren receive their shares, if any.
- Instead of age, you can tie access to periods of time, such as giving the child a portion of principal upon your death, followed by another portion 5 and 10 years down the line.
- You can define what type of payments you want the trustee to make on your beneficiary's behalf, such as for education, health care, or housing expenses.
- You can create incentives so that the beneficiary receives assets when a certain goal is achieved, such as attaining a college degree.
- If you have a beneficiary with special needs, you have to ensure that his lifetime needs will be taken care of by a trustee, above and beyond what the government provides, and without resulting in a monetary disqualification of benefits. We'll cover these supplemental special needs trusts in detail in chapter 12.
- You can grant broad rights to the money, but remember that even if you trust your heirs to use it properly, expanding the rights of withdrawal can give creditors and spouses easier access and cost the trust its ability to skip to your grandchildren's generation for estate tax purposes.

Dealing with Personal Property

Most families can divide personal possessions without too many ugly feelings or bloodshed. Unfortunately, that's not always the case. It's not always a matter of money; sometimes multiple descendants simply want to inherit the same treasured memento. I've heard of families coming to blows over a single photo album.

The solution to this problem varies from family to family. Many people prefer to let the beneficiaries decide among themselves who gets what. If they cannot agree, they can:

1. sell the items they cannot agree upon and split the money
2. donate the contested items to charity
3. let the executor or trustee decide who gets what

You *can* specifically bequeath each item to a particular individual through your will or revocable living trust, but this requires considerable detail. Besides, are you going to change your will or trust every time you acquire something new or give something away while you are still alive? One compromise is to maintain a separate list, which you mention in your will or trust, that details how you want your personal items distributed. You can change the list anytime you want.

This is also a good place to mention any particular items that you'd prefer to see go to a close friend rather than your family.
You can also:

1. videotape your possessions and narrate who gets what
2. set up a "round robin" to allow the beneficiaries to choose items for themselves, each selecting one item per round, as you would choose up sides for a neighborhood baseball game. Specify whom you'd like included in this process and perhaps who goes first. Is it just your

children? What if one of your children predeceases you? Should that child's children then participate in the division? What about your siblings or any close friends and relatives?

Consulting Descendants about Personal Property

Some experts advise those doing estate planning to ask their children which items of personal property they might want. The theory is that it's better to sort such issues out ahead of time, rather than create potential squabbles later.

This may well work for your family, but there's a trap here. Some children don't like to think about their parents' death. Others don't want to show any interest for fear that they will seem greedy. Some kids may start battling right from the get-go. As a result of any of these pitfalls, the entire estate-planning process might stall. If you attempt to sort out your personal property with the assistance of your children and they delay the process, move on. Don't let their procrastination be your downfall.

REAL-LIFE STORIES

Twelve years ago, Joyce died, leaving a husband, Henry, 52, a daughter, Emily, 17, and a son, Tom, 14. She also left an impressive collection of heirloom jewelry handed down from mother to daughter. When Joyce died, Henry took control of the jewelry, with every intention of passing it along to Emily when she wed, as Joyce had directed. But before Emily married, Henry remarried, then died without a will. Joyce's jewelry was divided between Henry's second wife, "the wicked stepmother," who received half, and Emily and Tom, who received 25 per-

REAL-LIFE STORIES

cent each. The stepmother gave her share of the jewelry to her own daughters. Tom couldn't care less about the jewelry and sold his portion. When Emily married and had a daughter a few years later, she did the necessary estate planning to protect what was left of her mother's heirlooms.

If you have substantial personal property that might be sold after your death, it might be worth your while to suggest a method of selling it. This is particularly appropriate if your children or the person in charge of liquidating the property understands neither its value nor ways to maximize that value.

Reputable estate sale companies and auction houses are very knowledgeable about dealing with such substantial assets as jewelry, art, antiques, or period furniture. If something might otherwise be sold for garage sale prices, leave instructions for your heirs to consult with expert resources.

The Pour-over Will

A fully funded revocable living trust might be a great estate-planning tool, but it does not stand alone. A complete estate plan also requires a durable power of attorney for property and for health care directives (both discussed in chapter 7), and a pour-over will.

A pour-over will is a special type of will used in conjunction with a revocable living trust. It "pours" any asset not titled in the name of your revocable living trust into your trust upon your death. As with all wills, it activates only upon your death.

The pour-over will does not need to be a complex document, but it should, like any other will:

1. revoke any prior wills
2. distribute any personal and household effects that have not already been distributed in your trust or elsewhere
3. appoint an executor
4. name a guardian for any minor children
5. instead of directing your estate to particular beneficiaries, the pour-over will directs the executor to transfer any remaining assets into your trust

Having a pour-over will as part of your comprehensive estate plan minimizes the impact of probate, while ensuring that your assets will be distributed in the manner that you state in your revocable trust. This is true even if you have not transferred all your assets into your trust prior to your death. However, when you have a revocable trust you want your will to do as little as possible. The more that the revocable trust is funded, the less work the pour-over will does.

Guardianship of Minor Children

You know that if you die without an estate plan, you'll have no say in who looks after your children in your absence. Your will, whether a pour-over will used in conjunction with a trust, or a traditional will, should name a guardian for any children who are under the age of majority—generally 18, but varying from state to state—or are disabled and unable to care for themselves.

Your selection of a guardian should be based in large measure upon lifestyle considerations. Who would impart the best value system to your children? Who would your children feel most comfortable living with? What living arrangement would be least disruptive to your children's everyday routine? These are the types of things that should be considered when selecting a guardian.

The selection of a guardian for your minor children is not an absolute right. It is actually a nomination made by you to the probate court through your will, with the court reserving final judgment over the matter. However, courts generally give considerable weight to responsible selections made by parents. As with all fiduciary appointments and nominations, it is good practice to name backups, in case the first or even second person(s) selected cannot act.

If your children have a surviving parent, that person will typically be appointed by the court *even if you nominate someone else,* unless there is a very substantial reason to defeat that person's parental rights—for example, if he is a criminal or a drug addict.

If you would seek to defeat someone's parental rights, provide as much information as possible to enable the court to make a ruling favorable to your way of thinking, but don't include anything that could be seen as a defamation of character, or your estate could wind up at the wrong end of a lawsuit. Keep it as specific as possible. Don't just make broad statements about the surviving parent's lousy character. Give hard facts that can be documented, such as court file numbers, arrests, convictions, and incarcerations.

Guardianship details people sometimes overlook:

1. If naming more than one guardian, you should determine what should happen if one of the guardians dies or, if they're married, the guardians split up. You can specify that you want them to act as guardians only if they are able to do so collectively, or that one or the other shall be permitted to act individually.
2. You might want your children consulted on the choice of guardian, depending on their ages at the time the decision must be made. Along those same lines, you might specify that an older child who has reached a predetermined age may act as guardian.
3. You may specify that a certain guardian shall act only if she is willing to take *all* of your children.

4. If religion is an issue, you might consider whether a potential guardian is willing to raise your children according to your religious beliefs (or to continue to expose them to the faiths of both you and your spouse, if different).

5. You might want to state specifically that both sides of the family should have generous access to the children.

Any of these things, and more, can be included in the will. Your ultimate choice of guardian can be based on any number of factors, but it doesn't need to be based on financial considerations. Your trustee can be instructed to make payments as needed so that your children are not a financial burden to their guardian.

Let's say your sister has a big house but you really prefer your brother, who lives in a modest house, as guardian. Your trust could be structured to pay for an addition to his house to accommodate your children. This could be a gift, or with a well-drafted estate plan could become part of your trust, which could be paid back later, when the house is sold. Your trust and your will (along with powers of attorney) should fit together as pieces in a jigsaw puzzle.

HOW TO DEFEAT PROCRASTINATION

Do the easiest part first so you can get moving.
Once you're moving—once you've made some decisions—it's easier to continue.

The guardianship decision comes down to personal preference. Who would provide the best lifestyle and give the most love to your children? If your children are young, who would impart the best value system? Obviously the answers to these questions are very subjective, very personal—and very important to your estate planning and to your peace of mind.

Should you name the same person(s) as both guardian and trustee? An argument can be made either way. It may be most convenient if the guardian is also the trustee. And, if you trust the guardian with raising your children, you should trust her with the children's money too, right?

Maybe yes, maybe no. The guardian is usually not required to provide too much detail regarding the day-to-day expenses related to your children, because keeping track of such items as the cost of food and other incidentals may be unnecessarily difficult. An allowance could be agreed upon between the guardian and the trustee, with additional requests being made for "big-ticket" items, such as private school tuition, orthodonture, or other large expenditures. For the big-ticket payments, the guardian would submit the bill to the trustee, who could pay them directly from the trust funds. Such items would be accounted for whether or not the trustee and guardian are the same person. If the same person has all the qualities to be both trustee and guardian, the only possible reason for their being different is if you feel the trustee should be keeping a close eye on everyday expenses and any resulting allowance for such items.

SHORT-TERM GUARDIANSHIP

Let's say you are going camping in a remote location for a week and leaving your children with Grandma. Your son falls on the playground and breaks an arm. Grandma might have a difficult time dealing with the emergency without specific permission from you to authorize your son's medical care. Illinois provides a useful form known as a Statutory Form for Appointment of Short-term Guardian. Check with your attorney: Does your state have a form that will accomplish the same goal?

Illinois Statutory Form for Appointment of Short Term Guardian
{Illinois Compiled Statutes 755 5/11-5.4}

(IT IS IMPORTANT TO READ THE FOLLOWING INSTRUCTIONS:

By properly completing this form, a parent is appointing a guardian of a child of the parent for a period of up to 60 days. A separate form should be completed for each child. The person appointed as the guardian must sign the form, but need not do so at the same time as the parent or parents. This form may not be used to appoint a guardian if there is a guardian already appointed for the child. Both living parents of a child may together appoint a guardian of the child for a period of up to 60 days through the use of this form. The parents need not sign the form at the same time.)

1.   Parent and Child. I _____ currently residing at _____
                        (name of appointing parent)   (address of appointing parent)
_____ am a parent of the following child (or of a child likely to

be born): _____
     (insert name and date of birth of child, or insert the words "not yet born" to appoint a short-term
               guardian for a child likely to be born and the child's expected date of birth)

2.   Guardian. I hereby appoint the following person as the short-term guardian for my child: _____ , currently residing at _____
                       (name of appointed person)   (address of appointed person)

3.   Effective Date. This appointment becomes effective: (check one if you wish it to be applicable)
(NOTE: If this item is not completed, the appointment is effective immmediately upon the date the form is signed and dated below.)

( ) On the date that I state in writing that I am no longer either willing or able to make and carry out day-to-day child care decisions concerning my child.

( ) On the date that a physician familiar with my condition certifies in writing that I am no longer willing or able to make and carry out day-to-day child care decisions concerning my child.

( ) On the date that I am admitted as an in-patient to a hospital or other health care institution.

( ) On the following date: _____ .

( ) Other:_____.

4.   Termination. This appointment shall terminate 60 days after the effective date, unless it terminates sooner as determined by the event or date I have indicated below: (check one if you wish it to be applicable)
(NOTE: If this item is not completed, the appointment will be effective for a period of 60 days, beginning on the effective date.)

( ) On the date that I state in writing that I am willing and able to make and carry out day-to-day child care decisions concerning my child.

Illinois Statutory Form for Appointment of Short Term Guardian
{Illinois Compiled Statutes 755 5/11-5.4}

( ) On the date that a physician familiar with my condition certifies in writing that I am willing and able to make and carry out day-to-day child care decisions concerning my child.

( ) On the date that I am discharged from the hospital or other health care institution where I was admitted as an in-patient, which established the effective date.

( ) On the date which is _____ (state a number of days, but no more than 60 days) days after the effective date.

( ) Other: _____.

5.   Date and signature of appointing parent. This appointment is made this

_____ day of _____ , 200 _____ .

Signed: _____.
                              Appointing Parent(s)

6.   Witness. I saw the parent sign this instrument or I saw the parent direct someone to sign this instrument for the parent. Then I signed this instrument as a witness in the presence of the parent. I am not appointed in this instrument to act as the short-term guardian for the parent's child.

Name and Address	Signature	Date
Name and Address	Signature	Date

7.   Acceptance of short-term guardian. I accept this appointment as short-

term guardian on this _____ day of _____ ,

200 _____ .

Signed: _____
                        (Short-term Guardian)

8. Consent of Child's other parent. I _____ , currently residing

at _____ , hereby consent to this appointment on this

_____ day of _____ , 200 _____ .

Signed: _____

(NOTE: The signature of a consenting parent is not necessary if one of the following applies: (i) the child's other parent has died; or (ii) the whereabouts of the child's other parent are not known; or (iii) the child's other parent is not willing or able to make and carry out day-to-day care decisions concerning the child; or (iv) the child's parents were never married and no court has issued an order establishing parentage.)

Action Plan Nine: You Can Make Good Decisions!

A four-step strategy for making key decisions:

1. Think about how you want your personal property divided among your beneficiaries. If you want to specify particular items, make a list this week. If you want input from the beneficiaries regarding what items they want, ask them to make their own lists. Although some of the beneficiaries might find the whole process to be morbid, consider targeting the next family get-together as an occasion to let them stake their future claims.

2. Decide on a system to resolve potential disputes over items of personal property that are not specifically bequeathed. You can direct that the trustee have the discretion to sell such items or allow the trustee to make the determination regarding who gets what.

3. If you have young children and have made your preliminary guardianship decision, discuss the decision with the person(s) you have selected, preferably before you sign your will. Make an assessment as to whether the prospective guardian is willing to act under the parameters that you wish. If your children are old enough, discuss guardianship issues with them.

4. Take some time to think through whether each of your beneficiaries can be trusted to receive their inheritances outright, or if some controls are needed.

CHAPTER 10

Looking Out for Estate Taxes

"In delay there lies no plenty."
—William Shakespeare

As you now know, those who fail to plan their estate let the probate court, which interprets state law, decide its fate. On top of that, without proper planning, the government might take a hefty slice for itself.

Thanks to estate taxes (death taxes), the government can tax your estate at rates close to 50 percent (or more), despite the fact that you probably paid income taxes on this money when you earned it.

The Old Law—The Unified Estate and Gift Tax Credit

Until 2001, the Internal Revenue Service allowed you to transfer up to $675,000—during your life or at death or in some combination—without incurring a transfer tax. That was above and beyond the $10,000 you were able to transfer to any person in a calendar year.

Another way of looking at that rule is that the government gave everyone a tax credit of approximately $220,000, often referred to as the Unified Estate and Gift Tax Credit, or simply the Unified Credit.

It worked like this: Upon your death, the IRS would add up all the gifts you made during your lifetime that exceeded $10,000 to any single person in any single year. Then they would subtract this figure from $675,000. The amount that remained was the amount that could pass through to your heirs without concern for estate taxes. The Tax Relief Act of 2001 changed some of the terminology, but left intact many of the strategies to maximize the Unified Credit and thereby avoid an estate tax.

Tax Relief Act of 2001

Under the Economic and Tax Relief Reconciliation Act of 2001 (the Tax Relief Act of 2001), estate taxes are scheduled to be eliminated after December 31, 2009.

So you think that you can ignore estate taxes? In a word, no! Even if you live through 2010, there is a twist—a "sunset" provision, whereby, in the absence of new legislation governing years after December 31, 2010, the estate and gift-tax law reverts to the current law. By then, there may be new laws, either retaining some form of estate tax, eliminating it, or just calling it something else.

Because we don't know what tomorrow might bring, it is smart to plan for estate taxes now, and if they are a nonfactor when you die, so much the better. Don't put off this tax planning just because you don't have an April 15 deadline staring you in the face.

Another change brought to you by the Tax Act of 2001 is the elimination of the stepped-up basis for capital gains purposes (see discussion in chapter 12) occurring after a person's death, scheduled to occur at the same time as the repeal of the estate tax (after December 31, 2009). Two exceptions are built into the new law—$1.3 million in capital gains designated by the executor and an additional $3 million designated by the executor to a spouse, which are both eligible for the step-up. Otherwise, the new law generally provides for a modified carryover basis, usually the original cost plus amounts spent to improve the asset. The basis on assets transferred at death will be the decedent's adjusted basis or its fair market value at the time of death, whichever is less.

The Tax Relief Act of 2001 provides the following estate-tax and generation-skipping (see chapter 13) tax rate schedule:

Year	Applicable Exclusion Amount	Maximum Estate Tax and Generation Skipping Tax Rate
2004	$1,500,000	48%
2005	$1,500,000	47%
2006	$2,000,000	46%
2007	$2,000,000	45%
2008	$2,000,000	45%
2009	$3,500,000	45%
2010	$0	NA
2011	$1,000,000	55%

If there's any chance that you, together with your spouse, might leave an estate worth more than $1 million, you should concern yourself with estate tax planning. To determine whether you and your spouse require estate tax planning, you must calculate the amount of estate tax that will be owed at the death of the second of you to die.

Estimate Your Federal Estate Tax

1. Gross Estate. Start with the value of your gross estate. Remember to include all your assets (see chapter 3). If no change is made to the current federal estate tax law (providing the sunset provisions take effect) and the value of the assets owned by you and/or your spouse is less than $1 million, there will not be an estate tax upon either the death of you or your spouse, regardless of the type of estate planning you elect. If your combined assets exceed $1 million, move on to Step 2. Note that there is no estate tax for people dying in 2010—referred to by some as the "throw Momma from the train" year.

   Example: Sam, a widowed man, owned assets with a value of $3 million at the time of his death. Sam had a mortgage on his home in the amount of $20,000. Sam's estate administration expenses were $10,000. Sam gave a gift of $210,000 to his daughter. Sam died with no estate plan.

2(a). From your gross estate, deduct your estimated debts, funeral expenses, and estate administration expenses upon your death.

2(b). The adjusted gross estate is further reduced by any assets qualifying for the marital deduction—that is, anything you expect to give a surviving spouse more or less outright. Then subtract from your adjusted gross estate any donations your estate will make to charity. The resulting figure is your taxable estate.

Example:	Gross Estate	$3,000,000
	Less Debts and Expenses	($30,000)
	Taxable Estate	$2,970,000

3. Add to your taxable estate the amount of gifts, if any, you have made since 1976 to any person in any given year that exceed $11,000 ($10,000 prior to 2002). These gifts figure in only if the total given to any one person in any one year is over $11,000.

Example: Taxable Estate $2,970,000
           Lifetime Gift to Daughter   __$200,000__
           Taxable Amount $3,170,000

4. Calculate your estimated tax due using the charts below.
   The amount of tax varies depending on the year you die.
   Any tax would be due nine months after the date of
   death. Refer to Internal Revenue Code section 2011 for
   more details.

   Example: The following is a calculation of the tax that
   would be owed if Sam died in the year listed below with a
   taxable amount of $3,170,000.

Year of Death	Tax Owed
2004	$786,600
2005	$774,900
2006	$538,200
2007	$526,500
2008	$526,500
2009	$0
2010	$0
2011	$1,038,500

Tax Rates for 2004–2011 and Beyond Estate Tax Chart for 2004	
Taxable Amount	**Estate Tax**
<$1,500,000	$0
$1,500,000 (but < $2,000,000)	45% on excess over $1,500,000
$2,000,000	$225,000 + 48% on excess over $2,000,000

Estate Tax Chart for 2005	
Taxable Amount	**Estate Tax**
<$1,500,000	$0
$1,500,000 (but < $2,000,000)	45% on excess over $1,500,000
$2,000,000	$225,000 + 47% on excess over $2,000,000

Estate Tax Chart for 2006	
Taxable Amount	**Estate Tax**
<$2,000,000	$0
>$2,000,000	46% on excess over $2,000,000

Estate Tax Chart for 2007 and 2008	
Taxable Amount	**Estate Tax**
<$2,000,000	$0
>$2,000,000	45% on excess over $2,000,000

Estate Tax Chart for 2009	
Taxable Amount	**Estate Tax**
<$3,500,000	$0
>$3,500,000	45% on excess over $3,500,000

There is no estate tax for people who die in the year 2010

Tax Chart for 2011 and Future Years	
Taxable Amount	Estate Tax
$1,000,000 (but <$1,250,000)	41% on excess over $1,000,000 (but <$1,250,000)
$1,250,000 (but <$1,500,000)	$102,500 + 43% on excess over $1,250,000 (but <$1,500,000)
$1,500,000 (but <$2,000,000)	$210,000 + 45% on excess over $1,500,000 (but <$2,000,000)
$2,000,000 (but <$2,500,000)	$435,000 + 49% on excess over $2,000,000 (but <$2,500,000)
$2,500,000 (but <$3,000,000)	$680,000 + 53% on excess over $2,500,000 (but <$3,000,000)
$3,000,000 and above	$945,000 + 55% on excess over $3,000,000

Note: The tax in each year at various asset levels is different from the amount you would find looking at the rate table in the U.S. Tax Code. The U.S. Tax Code first calculates the tax and then, in a separate calculation, deducts the applicable exclusion amount. The tables above have combined these calculations to make them more understandable.

This final figure should provide an estimate of your potential estate tax liability, at least given your current financial state of affairs. The value of your estate could obviously rise or fall between now and the time of your death, and federal or state estate tax law may change. The most likely tax law change may come from the state governments as the phaseout of the state death tax credit diminishes state revenues in "pickup" tax states. (See the discussion below regarding state estate taxes.)

Congratulations. If you have made it this far, take a break. You are doing a great job. Appreciate the gift of life and do something you enjoy.

State Estate Taxes

About forty states confuse the estate tax picture still further with so-called pickup taxes, which are also being phased out as part of the Tax Relief Act of 2001. In those states, your estate may pay pickup taxes that do not add to your total tax burden, via a credit on the federal estate tax return for state estate taxes paid as a result of death.

In 2002, states began to lose this credit, and the pickup tax credit will be completely phased out by 2005. This results in less revenue to pickup tax states. This phaseout of the state credit will make pickup taxes obsolete. The IRS will instead give taxpayers a deduction (before applying the federal estate tax rate schedule), rather than a credit, for estate taxes paid.

At least some of the states that currently benefit from a pickup tax (such as California, to the tune of about $1 billion per year) may make up the expected revenue loss by joining such states as Mississippi, New York, Ohio, and Oklahoma in taxing estates directly. Some pickup tax states have already "decoupled" their estate tax levies (with more in the process of doing so), severing the link between their taxes and the federal estate tax. Some of the states have even kept their annual exclusion amount equal to what it would have been under the federal law prior to 2001 ($850,000 in 2004, $950,000 in 2005, and $1,000,000 in 2006 and therafter). This means that even if no federal estate tax is owed at the time of your death, your estate may owe a state estate tax depending on whether your state of residence has decoupled and the form of the legislation your state enacts in its place.

Depending on the federal estate tax landscape and how various states react to the revenue loss, this could cause migration by wealthy people to the states whose estate tax climate is most advantageous.

HOW TO DEFEAT PROCRASTINATION

Consider the cost of putting the task off.
What future problems or unnecessary expenses might be created *now* because you are not taking care of current business?

The Unlimited Marital Deduction

One way to postpone estate taxes is the unlimited marital deduction, because gifts or bequests between spouses can exceed the maximum applicable exclusion amount.

You can transfer any amount of money, tax-free, either during your lifetime or at your death, to your surviving spouse—providing that the receiving spouse is a U.S. citizen, and that you are legally married, not living together as if married. Although the Unlimited Marital Deduction is referred to as a deduction, it more accurately might be called a blanket exclusion from all transfer taxes between husband and wife.

The primary problem with the Unlimited Marital Deduction lies in its overuse. When people learn they can leave their estates to their spouses without concern for estate taxes, they often assume this is the best option for most or all of their assets.

In fact, most married people have very simple estate plans. Their estate is structured so that upon one's death, all assets go outright to the surviving spouse. This is often referred to as an "I love you" plan, but it also might be called a myopic plan. In effect, the couple may be overutilizing their Unlimited Marital Deductions to the detriment of their other heirs.

It's a classic procrastination trap: Overuse of the Unlimited Marital Deduction doesn't avoid estate taxes. It only puts them off until the second spouse dies—when the problem may become considerably more difficult to solve. This is because the maximum applicable exclusion amount of the first spouse to die can be underfunded or lost. Taking the time to understand the system before either spouse dies can save taxes.

Consider this example: A man and his wife have an estate worth $3.5 million when the husband dies, bequeathing his entire estate to his wife. For the purposes of this example, we'll assume that his death occurs in 2004, thus qualifying him for a $1.5 million applicable exclusion from estate tax. His $1.75 million half of the estate passes to his wife. There is no estate tax at this point, despite the size of the estate, since the money is passing between spouses. So far, so good.

But what happens when the wife dies in 2005? The wife can't use the marital deduction, since she's no longer married. True, it's possible that she might remarry, but even then it seems unlikely she (let alone her dead husband) would want to leave all her money to a new spouse and none to her children by the first marriage. She can take advantage of her $1.5 million estate-tax exclusion amount—but the remaining $2 million of her assets will face estate taxes at a rate of 47 percent. This is avoidable. If the couple had planned ahead and taken even the simplest measures prior to the death of either, each partner's exemption could have been preserved and estate taxes completely avoided.

QDOT FOR FOREIGN SPOUSES

If the surviving spouse is not a U.S. citizen, she cannot benefit from the unlimited marital deduction. The U.S. government wants to prevent the surviving spouse from returning to her home country with an untaxed inheritance. Instead of being allowed to make unlimited gifts to a noncitizen spouse, the yearly maximum limit is $114,000.

Any assets over $1.5 million; ($2 million in 2006, 2007 and 2008; $3.5 million in 2009; $1 million in 2011 and there-

QDOT FOR FOREIGN SPOUSES

after) passed to a noncitizen spouse must be put into a Qualified Domestic Trust, or QDOT, that names a domestic trustee for the assets. (If the surviving spouse becomes a citizen within nine months after the death of the first spouse, a QDOT is unnecessary, but it ordinarily takes longer than nine months to process citizenship.)

Upon the death of the surviving spouse, assets in a QDOT will be subject to estate taxes.

Applicable Exclusion Amount Shelter Trusts

With a little planning, you and your spouse can conceivably shield a combined estate of $3 million from death taxes ($4 million in 2006, 2007, and 2008; $7 million in 2009; $2 million in 2011 and thereafter).

Your first planning move should be to consider structuring the estate to preserve each spouse's maximum applicable exclusion amount. The techniques described here are the most commonly used strategy by the reasonably affluent to minimize estate taxes.

Prior to 2002, this was done using a Credit Shelter Trust. Under the terminology of the Tax Act of 2001, the proper terminology is an Applicable Exclusion Amount Shelter Trust. But it may take a long time for the new terminology to take root, even among estate planning professionals, and anyway, the Sunset provision may once again make Credit Shelter Trust the proper term after 2010.

Whether you refer to it as a Credit Shelter Trust or as an Applicable Exclusion Amount Shelter Trust (let's just call it a shelter trust from now on), a shelter trust enables a married couple to fully utilize both spouse's maximum applicable exclusion amount and pass as much as $3 million ($4 million in 2006, 2007, and 2008; $7 million in 2009; $2 million in 2011 and thereafter) on to their children, grandchildren, or whomever they like, without any estate taxes. If they fail to plan ahead, they will be unable to preserve the maximum applicable exclusion amount of the first spouse to die, an all too common mistake.

The tax savings to your heirs can easily run into the hundreds of thousands of dollars.

Shelter trusts work like this: First, the spouses sever most joint tenancies. That means major assets previously owned jointly by both spouses are now owned by either one or the other, in trust or individually. Contact the financial institutions where your major accounts are held for instructions on severing joint tenancies, and ask your lawyer for instructions on dealing with other major assets, such as real estate.

Each spouse should individually control a basket of assets roughly equal to the current year's applicable exclusion amount.

The remainder of the estate can be held in either spouse's trust or in any way that seems most appropriate, perhaps in joint tenancy (although that can subject the estate to eventual probate upon the death of the survivor) or by some other entity.

Don't let your desire to hold a checking account or your automobile in joint tenancy with your spouse or other family member prevent you from setting up a trust. It's okay to continue to hold a few relatively minor assets, such as a modest joint checking account, in joint tenancy.

When the first spouse dies, his basket of assets, up to the applicable exclusion amount, will pass into a shelter trust, discussed below.

Estate Taxes—Shelter Trusts vs. Joint Tenancies—$3 Million Combined Estate

	All assets held in joint tenancy between spouses		Two shelter trusts with one-half assets owned by each trust	
Taxable amount at death of spouse #1		$1,500,000		$1,500,000
Deduct shelter amount* Amount flowing to Spouse #1's shelter trust (the applicable exclusion amount)	2004–2009 2010 2011+	$0 None $0	2004–2009 2010 2011+	$1,500,000 None $1,000,000
Deduct unlimited marital deduction at death of spouse #1 **	2004–2009 2010 2011+	$1,500,000 None $1,500,000	2004–2009 2010 2011+	$0 None $500,000
Calculation of tax on death of spouse #1		$0		$0
Taxable estate at death of spouse #2 (second to die)	2004–2009 2010 2011+	$3,000,000 None $3,000,000	2004–2009 2010 2011+	$1,500,000 None $2,000,000
Tax at death of spouse #2	2004 2005 2006 2007–2008 2009–2010 2011	$705,000 $695,000 $460,000 $450,000 $0 $945,000	2004 2005 2006 2007–2008 2009–2010 2011	$0 $0 $0 $0 $0 $435,000

*The shelter amount (the amount flowing to spouse #1's shelter trust) equals the applicable exclusion amount for the year of death. In the above example, for the years from 2004 to 2009, the total taxable amount equals $1,500,000. This will be the amount flowing to the shelter trust in our example even though the applicable exclusion amount is higher in later years. See chart at page 131. In 2010, the applicable exclusion amount is $0. In 2011 or later, the applicable exclusion amount (the shelter amount) is $1,000,000.

**The unlimited marital deduction usually equals the amount of assets flowing to spouse #2 at the death of spouse #1. When you have a shelter trust, the marital deduction is used to shelter any amount owned by spouse #1's trust that exceeds the applicable exclusion amount and excludes that amount from being taxed upon the death of spouse #1.

The term "applicable exclusion amount shelter trust" best describes its function, although the term "family trust" is what you will ordinarily see in a trust document that utilizes the shelter trust technique. The surviving spouse can benefit from the assets in the shelter trust during her lifetime, and can have significant, though not total, control over its assets.

If kept properly segregated, these assets never become part of her estate, and upon her death, the assets in the shelter trust are distributed in accordance with the wishes of her husband (the first spouse to die). In this way, the estate-tax exemption of the first deceased spouse can be preserved, provided the surviving spouse followed the trust's directions and did not commingle the shelter trust assets with other assets.

A few other details need to be considered: It might be necessary to change beneficiary designations of contractual assets, such as insurance. And careful thought must be given to the beneficiary designations of qualified plans, such as IRAs. Retirement plans in estate planning are covered in more detail in chapter 13. Your lawyer and other financial advisers can provide guidance here.

Technically, it is not necessary that each spouse's "basket" of assets be held in revocable living trusts during their lifetimes. You could, after dividing your joint tenancies, hold everything individually in your respective individual names, putting shelter language in your respective wills.

But I'd still recommend revocable living trusts for all the avoidance-of-probate reasons we detailed in chapter 8. In fact, revocable living trusts make even more sense here. Without them, the estate will face not just one probate, but two—one for each spouse's basket of assets.

Surviving Spouse's Authority over an Applicable Exclusion Amount Shelter Trust

The surviving spouse cannot have unlimited power over the shelter trust assets. If she did, the IRS would consider those assets to be part of her estate and the estate-tax benefits would be lost upon her death. The question most often asked here is. What are the maximum rights the surviving spouse can have over the deceased spouse's shelter trust without such assets being included in the survivor's estate? To give the surviving spouse maximum power (but not so much "control" that the shelter trust is included in her estate), the shelter trust may include such provisions as:

- She is the trustee and therefore can make all investment decisions.
- She has a right to all of the income from the shelter trust.
- She has a right to withdraw annually as much as 5 percent or $5,000 from the principal, whichever is greater. (This doesn't mean she should. In fact, if the estate is fairly large, it's generally best that this "five-plus-five power" not be utilized or even included in the trust. Even if not withdrawn, 5 percent of the principal will be included in the surviving spouse's estate.
- She has the power, during her lifetime or by her will (testamentary), to make gifts to descendants of the deceased, so long as such gifts are not used to discharge her legal obligation to support such descendants. The authority to make gifts granted under this type of "limited" power of appointment may extend to gifts to others, such as persons married to descendants of the deceased spouse, the deceased spouse's extended family, charities, or others.

- She can receive additional money from the trust if she is in need. If the surviving spouse spends all her money, including the marital trust assets, has received the income and 5 percent of the principal of her deceased spouse's shelter trust (assuming a five-plus-five power is included in the shelter trust), and still needs more money, the trust can provide for greater withdrawals, as specified; for example: to be used for her health and maintenance in reasonable comfort, or for emergencies. This provision is designed to ensure the deceased spouse's wish that the surviving spouse's standard of living be maintained.

It is usually best to leave the principal intact unless the surviving spouse needs money. Further, if there is an existing marital trust, the trustee is often required to deplete that trust before distributing principal to the surviving spouse.

With larger estates, the odds are good that the surviving spouse will have more than enough to live on even without any of the funds in the shelter trust. When a surviving spouse takes money out of a shelter trust, she might be undermining the estate tax advantages of the trust.

Left in the trust, these assets and any growth or income they produce should pass on to their ultimate beneficiaries free of estate taxes. Whenever possible, in a large estate, the best idea is to let the shelter trust grow. If successful investments within the trust have increased from its initial value, say from $2 million to $10 million by the time the surviving spouse dies, then the entire $10 million passes to the descendants free from estate tax.

A surviving spouse should take money from a shelter trust only when she doesn't have any other assets to spend. That said, it may be prudent for the surviving spouse to concentrate on investments that grow rather than produce income, because income retained in the trust will be subject to income tax, possibly at a higher rate than she would pay if the income were paid to her.

Also note that the level of spousal control over the assets in the shelter trust is discretionary. If the surviving spouse has more than enough to live on without touching the shelter trust's basket of assets, the trust can provide the surviving spouse with less authority or even none.

In this way, the trust might provide for the surviving spouse if her financial situation became desperate, for some unforeseen reason, but otherwise preserve the assets for the children.

Disclaimer Trust—Creating the Shelter Trust Postmortem

Although the surviving spouse's use of the shelter trust can be very flexible, it is still somewhat restricted, as assets owned by the shelter trust must be maintained separately and accounted for. Also, a primary residence owned by the shelter trust that has appreciated since the death of the first spouse will not receive favorable income tax treatment upon a sale.

Are there some cases in which you might make the surviving spouse's control complete? Yes, where there is what I refer to as a commonality of interests, when there is no reason to think that the surviving spouse will act against the wishes of the first spouse to die (as in leaving money to anyone contrary to the wishes of the predeceased spouse).

A couple with commonality of interests typically has no other children than the children they had together; built their estate together; and (absent estate tax considerations) intend for the surviving spouse to be the sole beneficiary of each other's estate. If either the husband or wife has children from previous relationships, there is no commonality of interests, because the surviving spouse tends to want to leave more assets to his or her descendants than to the descendants of the deceased spouse. Another example would be when there is a great disparity in age and/or wealth between the husband and wife, or if there are no children and each spouse wants different ultimate beneficiaries.

But in those cases where there is a commonality of interests between the spouses and a fading threat of estate taxes, why not make the surviving spouse's authority complete? There is a way—through the creative and timely use of disclaimers.

This is how it works: Assets are still divided between "his trust" and "her trust." The sole beneficiary of each trust is the other spouse. However, the surviving spouse can disclaim—that is, legally declare, "I don't want to own the assets of that trust (or a portion of the assets)." Any portion legally disclaimed within nine months of death flows into a shelter trust with the same authority to the surviving spouse that is permitted in any shelter trust.

The advantage to using a disclaimer trust is that the surviving spouse can be the one to decide, postmortem, how much money to put into the shelter trust instead of that decision being made prior to the death of the first spouse. The decision can be based upon advice given at that time, and based upon the changing estate-tax law and other circumstances that exist at that time.

The surviving spouse may, in fact, not disclaim at all, in which case she owns all of the deceased spouse's trust assets outright. Or the surviving spouse can still do estate-tax planning by deciding the amount that is sheltered. This is the ultimate in estate-tax flexibility for married couples with a commonality of interests!

Note: This type of planning may not work as expected if either spouse is, or becomes, untrustworthy or unstable.

The Marital Trust

If a spouse's basket of assets is worth in excess of the applicable exclusion amount ($1.5 million in 2004 or 2005; $2 million in 2006, 2007, and 2008; $3.5 million in 2009; $1 million in 2011 and thereafter) when the first spouse dies, upon his death, the amount above and beyond the amount put into the shelter trust may pass into a second trust, known as a marital trust.

For example, if a couple has a total of $3.5 million in assets, evenly divided between them at $1.75 million apiece, when the first spouse dies in 2004, $1.5 million passes into a shelter trust, $250,000 into a marital trust. (If the couple has only $3 million in assets or less, and those assets are evenly divided, then a marital trust would not be utilized.)

The marital trust benefits the surviving spouse and utilizes the unlimited marital deduction. Unlike the shelter trust, the marital trust may be structured so the surviving spouse has total control over the assets in the trust and can withdraw as much as she wants for any purpose.

Alternatively, a marital trust can be structured as a qualified terminable interest in property trust, or Q-TIP trust, which limits the rights of the surviving spouse. As with other marital trusts, Q-TIPs avoid immediate estate taxes by utilizing the unlimited marital deduction. Moreover, the surviving spouse *must* receive any income that's generated by the trust during her lifetime and, under certain circumstances, depending upon how the Q-TIP is drafted, may receive some portion of the principal as well.

But a Q-TIP trust also preserves the bulk of the assets in the trust for a different beneficiary after the surviving spouse's subsequent death. This can be useful when, for example, the surviving spouse is a second spouse, and the grantor wishes to support the surviving spouse during the remainder of her lifetime, then leave the money to his children from his first marriage.

Unlike Q-TIP trusts, other marital trusts may give the surviving spouse a general power of appointment—that is, they're structured to give the surviving spouse complete authority to withdraw assets from it. Such trusts basically become conduits for transferring assets estate-tax free to a surviving spouse once the shelter trust has been filled. In effect, it's as if assets distributed to the marital trust are given outright to the surviving spouse. And, in fact, they can be.

Some attorneys dispense entirely with the general-power-of-appointment marital trust (using a marital trust only if there are

Q-TIP provisions) and in the trust document leave the assets that would fund such a trust directly to the surviving spouse. I prefer keeping the general-power-of-appointment marital trust in the document in case the surviving spouse is not competent. Then at least there is a trust framework to handle the assets. Regardless of how the marital trust is structured (Q-TIP or general power of appointment), all the trust's income must be paid to the surviving spouse if the trust is going to successfully make use of the unlimited marital deduction and not face immediate estate taxes upon funding. That means without restrictions. For instance, you cannot say that she gets the income only until she remarries. That type of provision invalidates the unlimited marital deduction.

Upon the death of the surviving spouse, her estate for tax purposes will include any assets remaining in the marital trust, as well as her own assets. Since there is no restriction on her withdrawing the assets in the general-power-of-appointment marital trust, many surviving spouses during their lifetimes simply transfer the non-Q-TIP marital trust assets into their own revocable living trusts.

Unless she remarries and creates a marital trust with assets exceeding the maximum applicable exemption amount, there will be an estate tax due on the value of her assets beyond the maximum exemption amount. Distribution of her estate is then directed by her own revocable living trust.

REAL-LIFE STORIES

Even the best estate plan can be derailed if you don't get around to discussing the details with other relevant parties. Greg and Karen used a shelter trust in their estate plans to protect a sizable estate. But no one explained to Karen that it's best not to take principal out of a shelter trust unless she had no other funds available. As a result, after Greg's death, Karen not

REAL-LIFE STORIES

only lived on the income produced by the trust, but often dipped into its principal and rarely touched her other accounts, even though they were considerable. When she passed away, nine years later, her heirs found that she left a sizable estate—but the assets in Greg's shelter trust had not grown over the years and, in fact, had shrunk. This was a shame, because the assets in the account would have been estate-tax free. Meanwhile, most of the saved assets outside the shelter trust were taxed. This could have been avoided if Greg had gotten around to explaining the details of their estate plan to Karen prior to his death or if she had consulted an estate-planning attorney after he died.

Action Plan Ten: You're Almost Finished!

A four-step strategy to follow up your basic estate plan and minimize your estate-tax liability:

1. If you haven't already done so, complete Questionnaire Two in chapter 3. Use that to roughly calculate your potential estate-tax liability as instructed in this chapter.

2. If you have a potential estate-tax liability, discuss estate-tax-saving strategies with your attorney when you meet with him.

3. If you have already completed your estate-plan documents, immediately begin retitling your assets by contacting your financial institutions and changing ownership of various items. If you are married, this may include dividing your estate with your spouse to maximize the potential benefits of

Action Plan Ten: You're Almost Finished!

your shelter trust (or disclaimer trust). At the same time, conform your beneficiary (or secondary beneficiary) designations on retirement plan assets and insurance policies. If you have an irrevocable life insurance trust, you will also have to change ownership of policies so that they are owned by that trust (see chapter 13). Retitling your assets is a very important step to make the most out of your estate-plan documents. Mark a one-week deadline in your calendar to contact all of your financial institutions. Mark a two-week deadline to fill out your forms and send them to the financial institutions. Mark a one-month deadline to receive confirmations from all the financial institutions that the changes are in effect.

4. If you have any new real estate deeds transferring ownership to a trust, file those with the appropriate county within one week after they are signed.

CHAPTER 11

Gifting as an Estate-Planning Technique

"Misers aren't much fun to live with, but they make great ancestors."
—Terry Glaspey

A simple method to reduce future estate taxes and accomplish other estate planning or personal goals is available to those who plan ahead. You can gift up to $11,000 annually (to be adjusted in small increments for inflation) to as many people as you like without incurring additional taxes or reducing your unified credit/applicable exclusion amount.

To accountants and estate-planning attorneys, this $11,000 gift is known as the annual exclusion gift. The beneficiary of this gift need not be related to you; he can be anyone at all. Sometimes such gifts are made to help friends or family members or simply out of generosity, but they also can be used as an estate-planning tool. Every $11,000 you pass on to your future beneficiaries or others in this way during your lifetime is $11,000 that won't face possible estate taxes after your death.

Two more advantages to gifting:

1. You'll be able to see your beneficiaries enjoying the money while you're alive.

2. If invested, the gifted money's growth takes place outside your estate.

Of course, an aggressive gifting strategy will be a serious factor only if you estimate that your estate will exceed $1 million (unless there are also nursing-home considerations, discussed in chapter 13), and it will be prudent only if you won't need the money.

Procrastinators take note: Once a calendar year is past, the opportunity to take advantage of that year's $11,000 exclusion is gone forever. You can't just go back later and make gifts for years you missed. This is an exclusion that rewards those who keep on top of their estate planning.

Increasing Annual Exclusion

The government has decided to increase the maximum size of the annual exclusion over time. These increases, however, will not be as dramatic as the increases in the maximum applicable exclusion amount. Under the new rules, the $11,000 annual exclusion will increase to keep up with inflation, but only in increments of $1,000. Unless inflation dramatically increases over recent levels, expect the annual exclusion to remain at $11,000 or close to it for a number of years to come.

If gifting does make sense for you, here are some techniques you can use to increase its power:

- You and your spouse can *each* make a gift of $11,000 to the same person; or you can make a joint gift of $22,000 (a "split gift"), in which case a simple filing must be made with the IRS, but there is no tax, penalty, or depletion of the applicable exclusion amount.
- If the person to whom you and your spouse are making the gift is also married, you can make a gift totaling

$44,000 to the couple each and every year, without incurring taxes or reducing your unified credit. In this way, a married couple with three married children can reduce their estate by more than $1.2 million over the course of a decade—quite a significant amount.

Gift-tax rates are also being gradually reduced, but a gift tax will remain in place for gifts during your lifetime (above and beyond the annual exclusion gifts) that exceed a total of $1 million. In the years after 2010, the top gift-tax rate is scheduled to be the top individual income-tax rate at that time—35 percent.

The Education and Health Care Exception

Payments for tuition and medical bills are treated differently from other distributions. Above and beyond the $11,000-per-person gift, you can pay the tuition or medical bills of anyone you like without triggering a gift tax, so long as the institutions are paid directly. You can't just give someone money with the intention that they use it for college bills. (Room, board, and books do not qualify for this exemption.) If you are a grandparent, this can be a great way to help your grandchildren with their education expenses while simultaneously removing money from your estate. With tuition at top colleges averaging $30,000 a year or more, such gifts can substantially reduce a taxable estate and help a beneficiary.

There is one hitch to the $11,000-per-person annual exclusion: A "present interest" in the asset must be given. A present interest means that the donee (the person receiving the gift) must immediately be able to use or spend it any way she desires. Such a requirement may be contrary to your purpose in making the gift.

But there are ways to satisfy this rule without giving immediate and total access. For example, let's say that you want to set up a college fund for your grandchild and donate $11,000 to the fund every year for ten years. You want the money to eventually be used for college or graduate school. Rather than just hand the money over to the child and hope your wishes are respected, you can use one of the following tools:

- A Uniform Transfer to Minors Act account
- A 2503(c) minor's trust
- A Crummey trust
- A 529 plan

Uniform Transfer to Minors Act Account (UTMA)

The principal advantage of an UTMA, also known as a Uniform Gifts to Minors Act account, or UGMA, is its simplicity. You don't even need a lawyer. All you need is the child's date of birth and social security number to set up an account with a bank, broker, or mutual-fund company entitled "[Custodian's name] as custodian for [minor's name] under the [name of your state] Uniform Transfer to Minors Act."

The custodian, selected by you, as donor, administers the UTMA assets until the child reaches a certain age, ranging from 18 to 25, depending upon the state where the UTMA is set up. You can name yourself as custodian, but it's not advisable: If you do and you die before the assets are distributed, assets in the UTMA account become part of your probate estate.

The first $650 in earnings from an UTMA are income-tax free for children under 14, and the next $650 is taxed at 15 percent, but income or dividends greater than that amount will be taxed at the parents' top marginal tax rate, regardless of who the donor is. For children over 14, earnings will be taxed at the child's own rate, which is usually the lowest tax rate, since few children have substantial incomes.

Two disadvantages to an UTMA account:

1. When the child reaches the statutory age of payout, she has complete control. You might have intended the UTMA to be used for college, but if the child wants to buy a car instead, she has a right to do so.
2. The UTMA may mess up college financial planning. Under federal financial-aid formulas, children are expected to contribute 35 percent of their savings toward college each year, which means that dollars in their name count heavily against them when applying for aid packages. Parents are expected to come up with a maximum of only 5.65 percent of their assets.

Minor's Trusts—2503(c)

A second option is the minor's trust, often referred to as a 2503(c) trust after the applicable section of the Internal Revenue Code. Gifts to this type of trust are deemed to be gifts of a present interest even though the beneficiary cannot withdraw income or principal of the trust until his twenty-first birthday, or sooner if the donor so provides.

Other requirements of a 2503(c) trust:

- The trustee must have unfettered discretion to use funds to benefit the beneficiary. For example, the funds cannot be restricted to paying educational expenses. If you select a parent of the beneficiary as trustee (for example, your grandchild's father), he cannot use the assets to discharge his obligations to support his child, such as providing food and shelter.
- Once a beneficiary has achieved the age of 21, he must have the right to decide who gets the assets upon the beneficiary's own death.

- Upon reaching age 21, the beneficiary can do whatever he wants to do with the trust assets. Many donors feel 21-year-olds cannot be trusted with control of a significant sum of money.

One partial solution: The 2503(c) trust can be set up so that the trust actually continues past age 21. To satisfy the IRS, the child must be given a window of opportunity of at least thirty days to withdraw the assets, starting on her twenty-first birthday. If the withdrawal right is waived by the beneficiary in writing, then the trustee can continue to control the assets, usually providing for staged rights of withdrawal at certain anniversary dates or ages. At least this way, you don't have to worry about the money once the beneficiary has signed the necessary document.

A less common 2503 trust is the 2503(b) trust. A 2503(b) trust is similar to the 2503(c) trust except that (1) all investment income from the trust must be paid out to the trust beneficiary as it is generated, (2) the difference between the value of the assets held by the trust and the value of the beneficiary's income interest does not qualify for the federal gift-tax annual exclusion, and (3) in contrast to a 2503(c) trust, the principal is not required to be paid to the beneficiary or subject to withdrawal by the beneficiary at age 21.

Crummey Trust

A third option is a gift trust with withdrawal rights called Crummey powers, which are also often associated with irrevocable life insurance trusts (ILITs, which are covered in more detail in chapter 13), the insurance policy premiums being the amount of the gift in those situations. A Crummey trust is more flexible than the 2503(c) trust in that it may be for the benefit of multiple individuals and can be more restrictive and creative regarding the use of the assets. Incidentally, the name "Crummey" is the name of the family that was the subject of a court case. It does not describe the feeling you get from all of the paperwork it generates.

Crummey trusts satisfy the "present interest" requirement by giving the beneficiary a limited power to withdraw donations to the trust in the year made. Generally, this power is exercisable only during a limited period of time of not less than thirty days each year. The power is noncumulative, meaning that if the beneficiary does not withdraw his allotment one year, the power of withdrawal over that year's contribution lapses.

Even contingent beneficiaries may be given Crummey powers. But proceed with caution: If the IRS believes that there is insufficient present interest or that there is some collusion or prearranged understanding that the power of withdrawal was never meant to be exercised, it may challenge the gift-tax exclusion of the trust.

Also, where there is more than one beneficiary, careful consideration has to be taken to avoid a taxable consequence to the beneficiary on the lapse of the power, when withdrawal is not made.

One disadvantage of the Crummey trust is the need to create a paper trail. Each year when a contribution is made, the trustee must send a "Crummey letter" to the beneficiary advising him of his rights to withdraw. The Crummey notice is similar to the 2503(c) waiver, except it is done more often if there are annual gifts. This can be a nuisance for those who hate a lot of paperwork.

For a procrastinator, the Crummey's annual requirements can be especially problematic. To make your job easier, and to be certain you'll get it done, ask your lawyer for a copy of the form you'll need to send. Make plenty of copies so you can fill in a few blanks, sign, and date them every year, rather than be forced to draft the document from scratch each time.

FLY ON THE WALL

Although the IRS frowns upon prearranged or sham transactions, one very popular estate-planning technique is nevertheless somewhat convoluted—the use of waivers commonly known as Crummey letters, in which beneficiaries are saying, in effect, that they understand that they have a right to take your contribution to a trust or the full amount of his or her share, but decline to do so. The whole concept of the Crummey letter walks the fine line between the IRS requirement for a gift to be a "present interest" and your desire to postpone a beneficiary's full use of the trust assets.

In the vast majority of instances, the beneficiary goes along with the routine, but what if he refuses? There may be subtle ways of coercing a person to sign the waiver. Let's listen in on this totally imaginary exchange between a gifting father and a 21-year-old son who is beneficiary of a 2503(c) or Crummey trust that delays the beneficiary authority until he attains age 30:

Dad: "Here, sign this waiver. It says you don't want the money now."

Son: "Actually, Dad, I think I'll just take the money now. I want to buy cool stuff."

Dad: "No problem, but if you don't sign, I can pretty much guarantee that you will never get another inheritance from me or your mother."

Son: "Where's the pen?"

529 Plans

A 529 education plan allows you, as donor, to channel your annual exclusion gift for educational purposes to benefit anyone you wish. There are no income restrictions and the plans vary from state to state. You can make five years' worth of annual exclusion gifts (currently totaling $55,000) for one person in a single year. If you were to die, however, any "unused" years would be attributed back to your estate. You get no income-tax deduction for making a 529 donation. However, the income and growth in the plan will never be taxed if used for qualified educational purposes. You can retain control over the 529 account and you can even change the beneficiary designation if the originally designated person does not use the money. There are generally no age restrictions, so the 529 plan can be used for adult education. For more information, you may also want to check www.savingforcollege.com, a Web site devoted to 529 plans.

HOW TO DEFEAT PROCRASTINATION

Do not be a perfectionist! Make your best effort at each stage—it's assuredly better than doing nothing at all—and keep moving ahead.

The Big Lifetime Gift

You can make gifts greater than $11,000 per year per person, but such gifts may be subject to gift tax. Rather than pay a gift tax, most people who make large gifts will use all or part of their applicable exclusion amount. Even people who have no applicable exclusion amount left often choose to make inter vivos (lifetime) gifts in order to remove future appreciation from an already large estate.

There is another advantage to lifetime giving: Under current rules, taxes are effectively less. While Congress at one time intended to create a unified tax system, it did not fully succeed. Gift tax is owed only on the amount of the gift, while estate taxes are owed on the amount of the estate—a figure that includes the funds used to pay taxes. The net result is a higher tax on testamentary (after-death) gifts.

Choosing the Right Assets for Gifting

As you may recall from the discussion of joint tenancy in chapter 7, gifts of appreciated assets made during your lifetime will be treated differently by the IRS than assets passed to heirs after death through your will or revocable living trust.

If you make gifts of appreciated assets during your lifetime— say, giving your child the house you've owned for years—then the recipient may have to pay capital-gains taxes on the entire profit made on the asset from the day you bought it to the day he chooses to sell. On the other hand, if he receives the house from you after your death, he would face capital-gains taxes only on its increase in value from the time he receives it to the time it is sold, a potentially huge tax difference.

Thus, it often is smarter to make lifetime gifts of assets that have appreciated little or not at all since you purchased them. Leave highly appreciated assets in your estate.

There are three possible exceptions:

1. Gifts to charities. When giving to charities, an income-tax deduction can be taken for the asset's full value on the date of the gift and no capital gain is paid. Your basis in the asset is irrelevant, so feel free to give highly appreciated assets to charities during your lifetime.
2. Assets where there is reason to expect even greater appreciation in the future. If an asset is expected to be worth much, much more by the time you die, it might be worthwhile to pass it along now, even if it has already appreciated.

3. If you die after December 31, 2009, transfers upon death are scheduled to be treated the same as gifts, using an adjusted carryover basis instead of the stepped-up basis. This could result in a lot of capital-gains taxes and a paperwork nightmare as your heirs search your records to find out how much you originally paid for something. Try to figure out the cost basis on Dad's AT&T stock he purchased in 1971, reinvesting all of the dividends ever since! It becomes more important than ever to keep good records. Also note that there will still be a limited step-up on $1.3 million in assets transferred to any individual as allocated by the executor, and a $3-million limited step-up allocated by the executor if the transfer is made to a spouse.

REAL-LIFE STORIES

If gifting makes sense for you to reduce your prospective estate tax, don't put it off. Charlotte, 78, had known for years that gifting would be a good way to decrease her taxable estate. But despite the urging of her financial planner and estate-planning attorney, who saw she clearly had more money than she would ever need, she delayed, concerned that if she gave it away, she might not have enough to live on. Finally, Charlotte's health took a serious turn for the worse.

She decided to make $10,000 gifts to each of her five children and each of her seventeen grandchildren and great-grandchildren, which theoretically removed $220,000 from her taxable estate. Unfortunately, Charlotte died the next day, before any of the checks had been deposited. Because the gift was not completed until after Charlotte's death, the IRS disallowed the exclusions, and the money was still part of her estate, subject to estate taxes.

The change in law could lead to some late-in-life "marriages of convenience" to shelter a greater amount of appreciated assets from capital-gains taxes. However, you must remember to keep the Sunset provision in mind—it could be that the step-up is lost only for people dying in the year 2010.

Note: Congress did not eliminate gift taxes along with estate taxes because it did not want to encourage high-income taxpayers to transfer income-producing assets to lower-bracket taxpayers.

Action Plan Eleven: Make Someone Happy and Save Estate Taxes!

A five-step strategy for making gifts:

1. Decide if you're certain—not just likely—to have money that you and/or your spouse won't need to live on. If so, aggressive gifting might make sense. If your estate is likely to face estate taxes, then gifting may have particular advantages.

2. Ask yourself whether the beneficiaries whom you intend to make gifts to are old enough to act responsibly with money. If there is no estate-tax purpose to making the gift, it might be wiser to wait until the beneficiaries mature. If you want to make an immediate gift but do not want the beneficiary to have full immediate use of the gift, consider using one of the trust vehicles described earlier in this chapter.

3. If you decide to make annual exclusion gifts up to $11,000 per person per year, whether outright or in trust, act now! Once a calendar year is gone, the opportunity for making annual exclusion gifts during that year is gone forever. If you are married, consider doubling the size of your gifts. At the same time, consider taking advantage of the education and health care exception.

Action Plan Eleven: Make Someone Happy and Save Estate Taxes!

4. If you want to gift an amount larger than the annual exclusion amount, remember that a gift-tax return must be filed, and the result will be a full or partial depletion of your applicable exclusion amount.

5. You can make gifts larger than the applicable exclusion amount, but a gift-tax return will have to be filed and a gift tax paid. An advantage is that all growth will occur outside of your estate.

CHAPTER 12

Special Situations and Additional Options

"Oh, well, no matter what happens, there's always death."
—Napoleon Bonaparte

A well-drafted estate plan must account for unique circumstances. In this chapter we'll take a look at some additional estate-planning techniques. Some of these techniques are relatively simple and commonplace, while others are more aggressive, expensive to create, difficult to maintain, and, now and then, challenging even for sophisticated estate-planning professionals to understand.

But don't let that stop you from reading on. If there's something that sounds interesting but seems a bit complicated, just make a note of it, and remember to discuss it with your lawyer. Don't get hung up and lose your momentum.

The payoff for looking into these additional strategies can be tremendous—if they fit your situation. They can offer additional levels of security, help ensure that your estate is dealt with precisely as you desire, and offer protection from unnecessary taxes. Some of the wealthiest people manage to reduce their estate taxes to a fraction of the amount they might have paid without this additional planning.

Who needs to be familiar with these strategies? In truth, just about everyone, from the reasonably affluent to the super-wealthy, from the Ward and June Cleaver family to the most dysfunctional family in your neighborhood. They can make sense if you:

- own a substantial life insurance policy
- wish to make substantial gifts to charity
- own a business
- hold a large percentage of your assets through a retirement plan
- have a larger estate than can be protected from estate taxes even after utilizing the techniques mentioned in chapter 10

Some other special situations may need to be considered by those who:

- have beneficiaries requiring special attention
- intend to disinherit a descendant
- have been married more than once or have children from a previous relationship
- would otherwise benefit from additional trust strategies

That's a lot of people—and you need to know now if you're among them. So please read on.

Additional Trust Options and Other Ownership Arrangements

A wide range of tactics beyond those already discussed has been developed for using trusts and other ownership arrangements to transfer assets. These strategies usually take advantage of tax savings while giving up varying degrees of control at some level. Some arrangements that often come in handy are irrevocable life-insurance trusts, intentionally defective grantor trusts, buy-sell agreements, family limited partnerships and family limited liability corporations, offshore accounts, grantor-retained trusts, qualified personal residence trusts, various charitable trusts, Q-TIP marital trusts, and generation-skipping transfers.

Irrevocable Life-Insurance Trusts

It is a common and sometimes costly misconception that life-insurance-policy proceeds are never subject to tax. Life-insurance proceeds are not ordinarily subject to income tax, but they *can* be subject to estate tax if they're within the insured's control.

If you own life insurance outright and your estate, including the insurance, exceeds $1.5 million ($2 million in 2006, 2007, and 2008; $3.5 million in 2009; $1 million in 2011 and thereafter), it will be subject to estate tax, the same as any other asset.

You purchased life insurance to provide for your dependents upon your death; the last thing you want is to diminish the support the insurance policy was meant to provide. With proper planning, life-insurance proceeds *can* be removed from your estate. By utilizing an irrevocable life-insurance trust (also referred to as an asset replacement trust or wealth replacement trust, or an ILIT), life-insurance policies can provide needed liquidity when estate taxes become due.

It works like this: The insurance policy on your life is owned not by you, but by a trust that receives the policy's benefits when you die. Your heirs are named as beneficiaries of the trust. Upon your death, proceeds of policies held in this manner are excluded from your estate. Often such policies are set up to make sure heirs have enough cash to pay any estate taxes, if necessary. But they may be a good idea for anyone with a large life-insurance policy.

To ensure that the insurance proceeds are not taxed in your estate, this trust must be irrevocable and you must not retain incidents of ownership, such as the right to use the cash value of the insurance policy for yourself. This can be a drawback if you are considering funding the irrevocable trust with whole-life or universal insurance containing large cash value that you want to use to supplement your retirement income. For this reason, and due to its relatively low cost, term life insurance often makes more sense if supplementing your estate income is your primary or only goal.

Once the ILIT is established, you can transfer existing policies to the trust, or the trustee of the trust can purchase new policies on your life, funded by your annual exclusion gifts of $11,000 per beneficiary (or $22,000 if your spouse is also making the gift).

If you transfer existing policies into the trust, be sure to repay any loans against the policy, or the proceeds may face income taxes. Also, you must live at least three years beyond the transfer date for the IRS to allow the policy's proceeds to be excluded from your taxable estate. With new life-insurance policies owned from the beginning by the ILIT, there is no three-year look-back.

Typically you, as grantor, will make gifts to the trust every year. The trustee, in turn, uses these gifts to pay policy premiums. The trustee must give notice of annual gifts to all of the beneficiaries. These Crummey notices (also discussed in chapter 11) include advising a beneficiary of the right of withdrawal for a fixed period of time, perhaps thirty days.

Married couples whose heirs could face a cash crunch brought on by estate taxes after the death of the second spouse should consider a survivorship life-insurance policy (also known as second-to-die insurance, death-tax insurance, or legacy insurance).

This option is especially appealing if the bulk of the couple's money is invested in nonliquid assets such as real estate or a closely held business, and the applicable exclusion amount has been or will be depleted. Upon a payout, there will be sufficient liquidity so that your heirs will not be forced to sell illiquid assets at fire-sale prices to pay Uncle Sam.

HOW TO DEFEAT PROCRASTINATION

Clarify your objectives. Procrastinators sometimes put off a task because they're not committed to its goal.

Feel sure of your decisions and comfortable with your objectives—and you'll be motivated to finish!

Another purpose of survivorship life insurance can be to endow your beneficiaries. A couple of very modest means, for example, asked me to set up a supplemental-needs trust for the benefit of their only child, who has Down syndrome. The trust was funded by a survivorship life-insurance policy payable to the trust upon the death of the survivor.

A survivorship policy is relatively inexpensive compared to insuring one life, so they were able to get more bang for their insurance buck to ensure that their son's needs would be met in future years if they died before he did.

How much life insurance is appropriate?

- If the purpose of the policy is to pay estate-tax bills so your heirs don't face a cash crunch, base the amount of insurance on the estimated size of your estate taxes. Ask your lawyer to give you a rough idea of how much your prospective estate tax is, and talk to your insurance professional.

- If the life insurance is intended for care of your dependents, the amount to buy should be based on their current and projected future needs. That means enough to pay their day-to-day expenses, monthly mortgage (or to pay it

off), car payments, future college costs, and other pre-
dictable expenditures.

- If your spouse has a high income, or you have enough
  saved that your family would be secure even without your
  income, perhaps life insurance is not necessary.

Establishing and Operating an Irrevocable
Life-Insurance Trust

Irrevocable life-insurance trusts must be handled according to
a precise set of rules to be acceptable to the IRS. Frankly, all these
steps can be a real pain. Many of those who have them wouldn't
have them—except for the considerable tax savings they gain.

Here's what to do for such a trust to be valid and successful:

1. The grantor—that's you—must send a copy of the trust
   to the trustee you selected.
2. The grantor or the trustee must apply for a federal em-
   ployer identification number using IRS Form SS-4.
3. The trustee must open a checking or money market account for the trust. When the grantor makes gifts to the
   trust, the money will flow into this account. The trustee
   will use this account to pay insurance premiums. Such
   premiums must never be paid directly by the grantor.
4. The grantor must transfer ownership of the relevant insurance policies to the trust and designate the trust as
   beneficiary of policies transferred to the trust.
5. If the trust is to be funded with a new insurance policy,
   the trustee must sign the policy application and make
   the initial premium payment.
6. The grantor must transfer any other assets being used to
   fund the trust into the trust.
7. The trustee must send notice to beneficiaries of their
   Crummey rights of withdrawal in any year when a

contribution is made to the trust. If the beneficiaries are under age 18, the notice should be sent to the child in care of the nongrantor parent and, as a precaution, to a successor trustee named in the document other than a parent, assuming a parent is the grantor. It is good practice to save the posted envelope(s) and staple them to the letter, providing proof to the IRS that the notices were sent.

8. The trustee must prepare and file annual federal and state gift-tax returns, if either is required.

9. The grantor must be sure that the trust always has enough liquidity for the trustee to make insurance premium payments.

10. The trustee must make generation-skipping transfer elections if the trust uses generation-skipping techniques.

Intentionally Defective Grantor Trusts

Intentionally Defective Grantor Trusts, known as IDGTs, are irrevocable trusts that exploit certain inconsistencies between income-tax rules and estate-tax rules. They allow you, as grantor, to shift an asset out of your estate for estate-tax purposes, while continuing to act as owner for income-tax purposes. By paying the income taxes, you shift even more assets from your estate.

In many instances, an IDGT is used to "freeze" the value of a closely held business interest or real estate and involves part sale (usually about 90 percent of its value) and part gift (the remaining 10 percent). The sale portion of the transactions may involve the use of a self-liquidating installment note over a number of years, or the note may be payable in installments with a balloon payment on the due date. The IDGT may purchase life insurance on your life, using an interest-only note, with payment of the principal becoming obligatory only upon your death.

Some savvy practitioners swear by these oxymoronic-sounding trusts.

Buy-Sell Agreements

Life insurance can play a role in the estate planning of a small-business owner through a buy-sell agreement.

Such agreements are contracts providing for the sale of the stock of a business upon the occurrence of a specified event such as the death, disability, or retirement of a major stockholder. A buy-sell agreement often sets the value of the stock or provides a mechanism or formula for valuation.

It can provide a ready market for the sale of the owner's shares by his estate, and offer stability to the business by avoiding unnecessary friction brought on by new shareholders. Buy-sell agreements are often funded with life insurance, the proceeds of the policy being used to finance the purchase of the shares upon death.

There are primarily two types of buy-sell agreements.

- A cross-purchase agreement provides that upon the retirement, death, or disability of one stockholder, the other stockholder(s) agree to purchase his shares.
- A stock redemption agreement states that the corporation agrees to buy the disabled, retired, or deceased stockholder's shares.

A buy-sell agreement is especially useful in businesses with restrictive ownership rules. For example, CPA practices can be owned only by CPAs, so a partner in a CPA practice can't leave his wife his share of the business.

TAKING CARE OF (FAMILY) BUSINESS

If you own a business, consider what you would like to happen to it after your death. Is it something you could pass along to a child? Are your children already involved in it, or are they settled in their own careers? Would it be wiser to sell the business upon your death?

Discuss the matter with other partners you may have. Would they be amenable to new coowners? To working with your children? To purchasing your business outright? A buy-sell agreement might clarify these matters.

Discuss the matter with your children. Do they have both the interest and the expertise to take over the business? Does each child get the same share? What if one child has worked with you for years at the business while another has not? If you decide only one child should inherit the business, should the other children get more of your other assets to even things up, or does this child receive the business in addition to an equal share of other assets?

Family Limited Partnerships and Family Limited Liability Companies

By placing assets in a family limited partnership (FLP) or a Family Limited Liability Company (FLLC), you can maintain virtually complete control over the assets while at the same time make gifts to your descendants. This technique may remove assets from your estate and may reduce future estate taxes. FLPs and FLLCs are available in most states, but some state laws governing both are considerably more favorable than others, so don't be surprised if your attorney uses one outside your own state.

Parents may use FLPs and FLLCs to transfer such assets as real estate, marketable securities, and interests in closely held businesses to their children. As general or managing partners, you and your spouse make all investment and business decisions regarding the assets. The partnership agreement (in the case of the FLP) or the operating agreement (in the case of the FLLC) contains certain provisions that result in valuation discounts of 20–30 percent or more, due to lack of marketability and lack of control.

Over time, you can transfer the FLP or FLLC shares or interests to your children, lowering the value of your estate and reducing the estate tax. For example, using an FLP or FLLC and taking into account discounts for lack of marketability and lack of control, $14,000 or more can be transferred, with the gift officially counting as only $11,000. This allows you to get more bang for your annual exclusion buck. Upon your death, the FLP or FLLC (depending on its provisions) could be dissolved and the assets distributed to the beneficiaries.

In addition, FLPs and FLLCs offer protection from creditors, because partnership assets cannot be subject to lien. They can be subject only to a charging order in which the income paid to the limited partners or members of the FLLC is all that can be grabbed by the creditor. Both FLPs and FLLCs are more flexible than corporations, which must be maintained very strictly to preserve liability protection to its officers or directors.

An FLP or FLLC may increase the likelihood of an IRS estate-tax audit upon the death of a partner or member, especially if it is difficult to see any purpose for its existence beyond tax savings. But if your estate is large enough and the benefit flowing to your family from the use of an FLP or FLLC partnership is significant, it may be a worthwhile technique—despite increased IRS scrutiny.

Offshore Accounts

Some people stash their money in countries that do not enforce judgments awarded by the United States or other foreign courts. For this service clients pay lawyers $10,000 to $30,000, plus several thousand dollars a year in maintenance fees. Some popular spots for such assets are the Cook Islands, the Cayman Islands, Liechtenstein, Gibraltar, Belize, Costa Rica, Guernsey, Vanuatu, and the Turks and Caicos islands.

Some foreign trusts can be set up so your assets don't even leave the country, but remain outside the jurisdiction of U.S. courts. Generally, this type of strategy will be effective only if these trusts are established prior to any known creditor problem. This requires a "superspecialist" to handle it properly—and defend you in tax court if the IRS decides to crack down on the arrangement.

Grantor-Retained Trusts
(GRATs, GRUTs, and GRITs)

A grantor-retained annuity trust (GRAT) lets you transfer assets from your estate to a trust at a discount from those assets' value, "freezing" the value in your estate. By using this technique, the IRS discounts the GRAT below its actual value. Because a GRAT requires considerable bookkeeping, and requires that you give up a significant degree of control over the asset, its use is appropriate only for large estates where estate taxes will have to be paid.

There are two requirements for obtaining the discount:

1. The grantor must receive an annuity payment from the trust for a fixed number of years, based upon IRS tables. This reduces the value of the gift to the heirs for tax pur-

poses, because the heirs do not have immediate full use of the GRAT assets. The longer the retained-annuity period, the lower the value of the remainder interest is in your estate.

2. The GRAT must provide that if you die before the end of the trust period, its assets revert to your estate.

If you die before your lifetime benefits are terminated under the GRAT's terms, the GRAT is included in your estate. On the other hand, if you outlive the termination date, the GRAT's assets are excluded from your estate. However, if the GRAT is "successful" (you outlive its terms), there will be no stepped-up basis on any appreciated assets, so your beneficiaries may have income-tax issues.

GRUTs (grantor-retained unitrusts) are similar to GRATs. The difference is that with GRUTs, assets placed in the trust are reappraised each year, and the size of the income received by the grantor adjusted accordingly. This might seem like a hassle, but it helps ensure that if inflation takes off, the income the grantor receives from the trust will increase. That could be important if the grantor is living on the income—but it also could shield less of the assets from estate taxes.

GRITs are grantor-retained income trusts. With a GRIT, the grantor receives the income generated by the assets in the trust for some preset period of time rather than an annual fixed dollar amount, as in a GRAT. Recent laws have restricted the usefulness and popularity of GRITs.

Qualified Personal Residence Trusts (QPRTs)

A QPRT is a special type of GRIT. With a QPRT, you can transfer your residence to a trust while continuing to live in it for a preset term of years. You will still be able to deduct your real estate taxes and mortgage interest on your income-tax return. At the end of the fixed term, ownership of the residence passes to the trust's beneficiaries, often your children. If you as grantor wish to continue living in the house at the end of the term, you can lease the residence from the trust's beneficiaries at the prevailing market rate.

The advantage of a QPRT: Since your beneficiaries receive no benefit from the gift during the term of the QPRT, the QPRT transfer is made at a discount from the residence's existing value for gift-tax purposes. And once the residence is placed in the QPRT, any appreciation in the value of the residence accrues outside your estate.

During the term of the QPRT, you can sell the residence and either replace it with a new residence or convert the sale proceeds in the QPRT trust to a qualified annuity. If you do sell, capital gains taxes on any appreciation will be due, although you could take advantage of the preferential Internal Revenue Code rules for capital gains on residences. Roll over any gain from the sale into a new residence to avoid the tax or use your $250,000 exclusion ($500,000 if married) as often as every two years. The IRS allows two QPRTs per person, so it's possible to use this device for both your principal residence and one vacation home.

A QPRT will help avoid estate taxes only if you outlive its term of years, and then you must rent your home back from your heirs if you intend to continue to live there. If you do not outlive the term of the trust, the QPRT will be more or less ignored and the value of the residence is included in your estate.

Like GRITs, GRATs, and GRUTs, QPRTs require substantial paperwork and are worthwhile only if the prospective estate-tax savings are considerable. In such cases, the QPRT can be looked at as a "win-tie" situation. If the QPRT property is included in your estate, your only loss is the professional fees associated with creating and maintaining it.

Charitable Deductions and Charitable Trusts

As with lifetime gifts to charities, donations to charities at death are deductible from estate taxes owed. The simplest way to make a charitable donation is to provide in your will or trust for an outright gift to a charity upon your death. Or you may utilize trusts, including the following.

A *charitable remainder trust* allows you as the donor to receive the income from the trust assets during your or a family member's lifetime, or for a set period of time, up to twenty years. Upon termination of the trust, usually upon your death, the assets pass to the charity. This technique works well with highly appreciated assets, because capital-gains taxes are avoided.

Assets placed in a charitable remainder trust are removed from your estate with a corresponding income-tax deduction for the value of the remainder—an estimate of the amount the charity will receive upon your death.

A *net income with makeup charitable remainder unit trust (NIMCRUT)* is a type of charitable remainder trust that allows income to be deferred to later years. Although the NIMCRUT requires a fixed percentage (at least 5 percent annually) or the income, whichever is less, to be paid to you or some other beneficiary that you choose, the NIMCRUT can invest in assets that, while increasing in value, pay little or no current income. The deficiency between the fixed percentage and the actual income is a tax deferral that builds up over time. Typically, NIMCRUTs are funded by tax-deferred annuity contracts that allow you to defer income until it is requested. If you do not need immediate cash flow, a NIMCRUT may work well as a charitable vehicle with income- and estate-tax benefits.

A *charitable lead trust* uses the opposite approach from charitable remainder trusts. A charity or group of charities receives the income from trust assets for a set term of years. When the term expires, the trust assets are transferred to your heirs.

Because a charity receives the income from your assets for a term of years, you are able to pass the assets to your heirs at a discount from the value of the bequest if all rights to the property were transferred at once.

A *pooled income fund* is offered by some larger charities. You donate assets to the charity, then receive rights to a percentage of the income generated by the charity's fund until your death (how large a percentage is based on the value of the assets you donate). Pooled income funds allow you to diversify your assets during your lifetime while benefiting a charity at your death.

A *family foundation* allows you as donor to retain personal control and flexibility over the donated assets. If properly established and administered, it can utilize all of the usual charitable income-tax deductions, while also providing for the long-term needs of the people and organizations you want to help.

During your lifetime, it can become a forum in which family members can work toward a common charitable goal. It can be structured so that, after your death, through good investing, principal may be maintained or increased over time, making an impact for generations to come.

Numerous other techniques, some of which are complex and involve varying degrees of loss of asset control, during your lifetime or following your death, can benefit charities while providing tax breaks to you or your family. If you would like to benefit a particular charity, it can be worthwhile to approach that charity and discuss creative ways to meet both your needs.

REAL-LIFE STORIES

Forward-thinking individuals, some of whom are fairly "ordinary," set up family foundations to distribute much of their wealth. Joe has a $5-million estate and two young-adult children.

Instead of leaving the children the entire $5 million (minus taxes), he decided to do something that makes sense tax-wise and in other ways too: He set aside half his fortune to create a family foundation. The children will get involved during Joe's lifetime and help manage the foundation as directors, working with various charitable projects.

This may lead to a greater sense of life purpose than if Joe just gave them the money to buy things or grow the portfolio. It could enrich Joe's whole family in ways that are more important than net-worth statements.

Ask yourself how much is enough. Does it make a big difference if a child gets an inheritance of $3 million versus $2 million? Inheriting large sums of money can sometimes do great damage to a person's character. The inheritor obtains a fortune he never had to work for, then possibly blows it, or—just as bad, in my opinion—the inheritance blocks his natural need to struggle for success, causing a failure to learn about compassion, work ethic, and empathy for those who are less fortunate. Certainly, doing good things for many people can be a greater legacy than just hoarding family money.

Perhaps you agree with Warren E. Buffett, the billionaire investor, who said it might be wisest to leave children "enough money so that they would feel they could do anything, but not so much that they could do nothing."

What's Best for Charity?

People often ask what assets are most suitable for charitable gifting. If you want to make asset gifts to charity during your lifetime, you get the most bang for your buck with appreciated assets.

This is because you will be able to take an income-tax write-off for the full value of the appreciated asset, but because the charity pays no income tax, it can convert the asset to cash with no adverse tax effect.

In contrast, if you make a lifetime gift of the same appreciated asset to a family member, for example, that person must pay capital-gains tax on the difference between its sale price when the asset is sold and its original value. Plus, you receive no income-tax writeoff. When gifting to individuals, therefore, you get the most bang for your buck with cash, cash equivalents, or any asset (such as stock options) likely to grow in the future.

Charities also make great beneficiaries for your IRA and other qualified plan assets, since these will otherwise be subject to both income tax and estate tax upon your death. The IRS recently enacted regulations making this a more favorable technique than in years past.

THE KRESGE STORY, BRIEFLY

In 1899, Sebastian S. Kresge opened a modest store in downtown Detroit. Eventually, Kresge's evolved into the giant retailer Kmart, land of the blue light special, with more than 1,800 stores and 220,000 employees. In January 2002, Kmart filed for Chapter 11 bankruptcy protection.

Meanwhile, in 1924, Mr. Kresge, with a personal gift of $1.3 million, began the Kresge Foundation, to "promote the well-being of mankind." Today, the Kresge Foundation grants

THE KRESGE STORY, BRIEFLY

support a broad range of organizations reflecting almost the entire array of the nonprofit sector. Since its establishment, the Kresge Foundation has awarded nearly 7,500 grants for a total of almost $1.5 billion.

To my mind, this illustrates that generosity can outlast the other good and great things we do throughout our lives. Leaving a charitable legacy perpetuates your good deeds long after you're gone.

Special Issues for Retirement Plans

The primary purpose of retirement plans, as the name implies, is to provide income for retirement. This is accomplished, in part, by income-tax breaks. Money invested in an IRA (or other qualified retirement plans, including 401(k), 403(b), and 457) is deducted from your gross income in the year that the investment is made, resulting in a lower income tax. Assets in the IRA grow tax deferred until they are withdrawn. The key is withdrawal.

You must begin to withdraw from your IRA prior to April 1 in the year following the year in which you reach the age of 70½ (70 years and six months). This is termed your required distribution date (RDD) and is based upon IRS actuarial tables. Unless you need the money to live on, you want to withdraw as little as possible, which defers income taxes as long as possible. Careful planning will help you accomplish that goal, especially following changes in the law that took place in 2001.

Many of the previously draconian provisions were removed at that time. Suffice it to say that until recent changes, rules governing the minimum required distribution (MRD) were impossibly complex. Now they are greatly simplified and usually will allow you to make smaller withdrawals, resulting in greater deferral and ultimately a lower income-tax bill.

The new IRA distribution rules made three key changes:

1. **Simplified and Smaller Distributions.** One simplified table, commonly used to calculate the MRD, automatically recalculates your life expectancy every year. The only exception occurs if your spouse is more than ten years younger than you. In that case, a different "joint and survivor" table is used.

2. **Payouts after Death Can Be Slowed.** Eventually, income taxes must be paid, if not during your lifetime, then at some point during the lifetime of your surviving beneficiaries. The key to determining this factor is whether there is a designated beneficiary, and if so, who it is.

   Without a designated beneficiary, the required payout of a person who has reached his RDD is calculated using his remaining life expectancy as determined immediately prior to the time of death.

   If the person who has no designated beneficiary dies prior to his RDD, the account must be paid out within five years of the date of the owner's death.

   With a designated beneficiary, the account balance may be paid out over the beneficiary's remaining life expectancy, even if you don't reach your RDD.

   A designated beneficiary is usually an individual, but it also can be a trust, if there are individual beneficiaries within the trust. With multiple beneficiaries, the age of the eldest beneficiary is the measuring stick to determine the MRD.

   In all cases, distributions must begin no later than September 30 in the year following your death. The IRS can penalize—up to 50 percent of the MRD— anyone who fails to withdraw his MRD amount each year.

3. **Designated Beneficiaries Can Be Changed.** Even after reaching the RDD, an IRA owner can change beneficiaries. Before the law was changed, the choice of beneficiaries made at that time determined the withdrawal schedule and was frozen forever. This is no longer true. After reaching age 70½, you can change your beneficiary. In fact, the designated beneficiary is not required to be named until the end of the year following the year of the plan owner's death.

The new laws regarding IRA beneficiary designations create greater planning opportunities. Beneficiaries can disclaim their inheritance of retirement accounts, charitable distributions can be made with retirement assets, and dividing the IRA into separate shares for each beneficiary can realign the amounts each beneficiary receives.

Naming a charity as beneficiary is now highly advantageous. Neither estate tax nor income tax is paid on a charitable bequest. Because your IRA is all pretax dollars, the savings can be significant.

REAL-LIFE STORIES

When Mark's mother died, leaving him a considerable sum, he made the smart move: He decided not to take the money. This is something that rarely occurs to those who have neither planned ahead nor discussed their options with a financial planner or estate-planning attorney, but it can make good sense.

What's the benefit of turning down a seven-figure windfall? Mark is already in his sixties, retired, financially comfortable, and has children and grandchildren. He doesn't need the money—but his children might. Had he taken the inheritance, it would have passed through his estate and on to his kids later—after another round of taxes, that is.

REAL-LIFE STORIES

By taking advantage of disclaimers, the inherited funds moved on to Mark's heirs, as if he had predeceased his mother. Those considering such a course should note that disclaimers must be made within nine months after the death of the decedent. Both during and after that nine-month period, the disclaiming party must not receive any direct benefit from the assets being disclaimed.

Selecting Your Beneficiary

Assume a husband and wife have a total net worth of $2 million. Of this total, $1 million is in the husband's IRA. In order to defer income taxes as long as possible and provide for his wife after his death, the husband should name his wife as beneficiary of the IRA. This will allow for a spousal IRA rollover if she survives him. She can continue to defer completely the income taxes during her lifetime until her RDD. This rollover feature is available only to spouses.

Naming your spouse as beneficiary of a qualified retirement plan can make sense from an income-tax perspective. But it can be problematic from an estate-tax perspective, if it wastes the IRA owner's entire applicable exclusion amount.

Remember from chapter 10 that it is possible for a couple to protect as much as $3 million ($4 million in 2006, 2007, and 2008; $7 million in 2009; $2 million in 2011 and thereafter) from estate taxes through proper use of a shelter trust, but only with proper planning.

If we knew which spouse would die first, all their assets, except for IRAs, could be in one trust, the trust of the first spouse to die. The IRA would name the other spouse as initial beneficiary. Upon the death of the first spouse, that spouse's shelter trust would be funded with $1 million of the couple's assets that are not in qualified plans, preserving the maximum applicable exclusion amount of the first spouse to die. The $1-million IRA would be rolled over by the surviving spouse, thereby deferring both income taxes and estate taxes.

However, a problem arises if the predicted sequence of deaths does not hold. The "basket" of the spouse who is first to die would be empty, sacrificing his applicable exclusion amount. Upon the survivor's subsequent death, taxes would be paid on the entire estate, minus only the survivor's applicable exclusion amount. If the couple's assets other than the IRA are divided equally, at least some of each spouse's applicable exclusion amount can be utilized.

Another option would be to put all the assets except the IRA into the wife's trust. The IRA would name the wife as initial beneficiary, with the husband's trust or descendants as contingent beneficiaries. If the wife dies first, her applicable exclusion amount trust basket would be filled. Upon the husband's subsequent death, his basket also would be filled. But what if the husband dies first? If the wife rolls over the IRA, his trust is empty.

This is one area where the strategy of disclaiming (refusing) assets can be a very useful form of postmortem tax planning. Disclaimers can be made for all or a portion of assets. The wife, together with her various advisers, can look at the ramifications of disclaiming all or part of the IRA. Assuming the husband's trust has been named contingent beneficiary of the account, this will partially or completely fill up the husband's shelter trust.

In this situation, the numbers should be crunched to assess the various tax implications. To the extent the wife disclaims the IRA, income taxes will accelerate, compared with her rolling over the IRA.

There also could be other excise or penalty taxes. Keep in mind that estate taxes on the first $1.5 million ($2 million in 2006, 2007, and 2008; $3.5 million in 2009; $1 million in 2011 and thereafter) of the first spouse to die can be completely avoided, while income taxes eventually must be paid on the IRA. Although the new liberalized rules allow survivors to "tweak" beneficiary designation up to the end of September of the year following your death, a disclaimer must be made within nine months of death.

Trust Wrinkles for Complex Family Situations

Not everyone's family is the same. Fortunately, trusts need not be one-size-fits-all documents. Strategically conceived and properly constructed, they're flexible vehicles that can accommodate virtually any family circumstance.

Here's a look at some potential complications and how trusts can be used to sort them out.

Disabled Family Members

If you are responsible for taking care of a family member who will never have the capacity to take care of himself, your estate plan must address the situation. You can make provisions to ensure that he will have the means to support his current lifestyle without giving him any money outright, if he isn't able to handle it or if government aid is a factor.

If the individual is legally disabled and receiving some type of governmental aid, a supplemental special-needs trust, or SSNT, is essential. An SSNT allows a trustee named by you to supplement whatever needs your disabled beneficiary has that are not covered by any governmental program. The SSNT is intended *not* to be used to provide basic food, clothing, and shelter, nor be available to the beneficiary for conversion for such items, until all local, state, and federal benefits for which the beneficiary is eligible as a result of disability have first been fully expended for such purposes.

The trustee should have the discretion to pay for quality-of-life expenditures such as:

- the cost differential between a shared room and a private room
- travel costs, especially to visit family members
- reimbursement for attendance at or participation in recreational or cultural events, conferences, seminars, or training sessions
- the cost of a companion or attendant necessary to make travel and similar activities possible
- elective medical, dental, or other health services not provided
- small, irregular amounts of spending money
- exercise equipment
- computer hardware and software; audio and video equipment including radios, television sets, and recorders; tapes, books, and movies; and membership in clubs purchasing such items
- subscriptions to newspapers and magazines
- money to purchase appropriate gifts for relatives and friends
- additional food, clothing, and other expenditures used to provide dignity, purpose, optimism, and joy to the beneficiary, such as a vacation

The payments referred to above are made directly or indirectly so they don't disqualify or interfere with government assistance.

Additional instructions may be given to the trustee (or someone the trustee designates) to visit the disabled beneficiary on a regular basis to inspect the beneficiary's living conditions and make certain evaluations, which may include:

- physical and dental examination by an independent physician and dentist

- an evaluation of the beneficiary's grooming and overall appearance
- an evaluation of education and training programs
- an evaluation of work opportunity and earnings
- an evaluation of recreation, leisure time, and social needs
- a determination of the appropriateness of existing residential and program services, and
- an evaluation of the legal rights to which the beneficiary may be entitled, including free public education, rehabilitation, and programs that meet constitutional minimal standards

Almost any trust can benefit from at least a minimal amount of SSNT language, because you never know when a beneficiary may become incapacitated. You may not want your trust to unintentionally cause the beneficiary to lose out on government subsidies that the beneficiary is entitled to receive.

The above discussion of SSNT assumes that it is funded by assets other than those belonging to the beneficiary. If it is funded by the beneficiary's own assets, then for it to be valid there must also be language that the government agency or agencies are reimbursed from the trust upon the beneficiary's death.

Minor or Spendthrift Family Members

Some heirs are temporarily or permanently untrustworthy with money. In the case of a minor child, it's probably just a temporary concern: You don't want to put all the money in the heir's hands until he is old enough to use it responsibly.

A trustee can be given discretion over how trust assets are spent for the child's health, support, education, and maintenance. The child may gain control over the trust in stages, such as a power to withdraw income at a certain age, followed by a right to withdraw one-half the principal five years later, for example, followed by a right to withdraw the balance of the principal five years after that. You may decide that the child should never gain full control. The influence you want to exercise from the grave is limited mostly by your imagination and how much you procrastinate.

Families in Need of Incentives

Provisions may be used in a trust to entice a beneficiary to do things you want him to do, such as:

- go to college
- attain a certain grade point average
- become gainfully employed
- attain a certain net worth through his own efforts
- get married
- invite his siblings to "life-cycle events" such as marriages, christenings, bar mitzvahs, or other occasions

Or such provisions may be used in a trust to entice a beneficiary not do things, such as:

- fail a drug test
- have children outside of marriage
- pierce his body in various places or cover it with tattoos

Trusts containing provisions of this sort are occasionally referred to as values trusts. Some may cringe at such provisions— they are, in effect, telling other people how to live—but some people do that their whole lives anyway: Why stop upon death? When placing incentives into your trust, make sure that the provisions are flexible, because what you think makes sense today may not make sense in the future. For example, if you were to say that a child *must* obtain a college degree for him to receive *any* assets, would that be appropriate if he became disabled and was unable to attend school? Also, any incentive (or disincentive) provisions should be readily verifiable by a trustee. Having children outside of marriage may be verifiable, while a prohibition on extramarital affairs could involve more than a trustee could stomach.

Provisions containing incentives usually can be enforced, but the court could dismiss those that are contrary to public policy. For example, a provision that your child not marry someone of a different race would be invalid because it is racially discriminatory.

Q-TIP for a Second Marriage

As we discussed in chapter 11, a Q-TIP is a type of marital trust that benefits a spouse during the spouse's lifetime without relinquishing the power to choose the ultimate beneficiaries.

Q-TIP marital trusts are most commonly used in second marriages. For example, let's consider a situation where both husband and wife have children from previous marriages. The husband wants to provide for his current wife should she survive him, but upon her subsequent death he wants the marital trust assets to go to his descendants from his previous marriage and not to her descendants.

With the Q-TIP marital trust, as with all marital trusts, the wife *must* receive all the income either quarter-annually or on a more regular basis. Upon her death, the property is distributed as her husband specified, presumably to his descendants. If the husband chooses, he can also provide for an unbiased trustee with the authority to distribute principal to the second wife as needed. Often, a Q-TIP marital trust will mirror the shelter trust, except that in the shelter trust, income can be retained or paid to someone other than the surviving spouse.

Generation-Skipping Transfers

Above and beyond estate taxes, transfers to grandchildren or more remote descendants can be subject to a tax called the generation-skipping transfer tax, or GST tax.

If you make gifts to a grandchild while the grandchild's parent (your child) is alive, you or your estate will face a highly punitive flat tax of the top transfer tax rate (48 percent in 2004, 47 percent in 2005, 46 percent in 2006, 45 percent in 2007, 2008, and 2009, and 55 percent in 2011 and thereafter), which is added to any gift or estate tax. This effectively allows the IRS to tax every generation.

Fortunately, there is a GST tax exemption, which is the same in any given year as the applicable exclusion amount.

There are many reasons to give a gift directly to a grandchild, including an estrangement from your child, the parent. Or perhaps you have plenty of money and simply want to spread it around the family. You can also give a gift indirectly to a grandchild using a GST trust. Perhaps your child is in danger of a major lawsuit or has a large estate of his own, does not need your inheritance, or believes it might compound his own estate-tax problems.

Shifting money to your grandchild might make sense. Using a GST trust, you can leave an inheritance under the control of your child (that is, the grandchild's parent), with the level of control by your child determined by you, the grantor. Of course, if the grandchild's parent (your child) is in a profession where he is at a high risk of being sued, or if he is notably bad with money, it might make sense to name someone else as trustee.

Proper use of a GST trust is akin to giving your children a gift of an additional exemption from estate taxes. If the money has been invested, the resulting growth is exempt from estate taxes in your child's estate.

An additional technique might be "spray" trust provisions

that would allow trust assets to benefit any descendant at any level, so that any child, grandchild, or great-grandchild can be helped according to individual needs.

The rates on generation-skipping taxes have been reduced along with other top estate-tax rates. The GST is scheduled to be eliminated with the estate tax in 2010, but the Sunset provision of the Tax Relief Act of 2001 could bring GST taxes back after 2010.

Disinheriting Family Members

Some people decide, often after considerable soul searching, that a potential heir does not deserve an inheritance. It is important that you not just ignore this potential heir in your estate plan. Instead, be very specific. For example, if you are making gifts to all your nieces and nephews except for one who turned his back on the family twenty years ago, specifically mention that nephew and your intentions. If he is ignored, he may be able to assert that you "forgot" about him.

If you wish to explain your reasons for excluding a beneficiary, keep it brief and unemotional—enough to get the point across without unnecessarily dredging up old conflicts. Some people get downright mean-spirited when disinheriting, utilizing the opportunity to tell someone "once and for all" what they think of him. Before you do that, keep in mind that if you commit an act of libel in your will, your disinherited beneficiary might be able to sue your estate and gain his inheritance (and possibly more) through the back door.

Disinheriting a spouse can be particularly difficult, because many states mandate a certain percentage of the estate for surviving spouses who assert their rights to take a spousal election. Let's say a husband is separated from his wife and leaves her only $10 in his will. In many states, she can renounce her share under the will and receive a percentage of the probate estate, often about one-third.

Traditionally, in many states, assets subject to a spousal election were probate assets only. Consequently, many disgruntled spouses structured their estates so the bulk of their assets would pass outside of probate, defeating any spousal rights.

Let's say the husband has a revocable living trust. The beneficiaries of the trust are his two children, but not his wife.

Besides the trust, he has the following assets:

- a bank account in joint tenancy with his daughter
- a brokerage account that is payable on death (POD) to his son
- investment real estate owned by his revocable living trust
- IRA and insurance policies that name either his children or his trust as beneficiary

In some jurisdictions the surviving spouse may end up with far less than one-third of the husband's overall estate. Some other states have reformed their laws to allow the surviving spouse to renounce an "augmented" estate, which includes *all* assets, including nonprobate ones such as insurance, joint tenancy assets, and other assets that would be considered part of a decedent's gross estate for estate-tax filing. Often, a case like this will be decided on the facts unique to the particular situation.

Prior agreements, such as prenuptials, may affect and even defeat a spouse's rights to an elective share. Also, there are technical steps that must be taken by the spouse who wishes to take an elective share, including strict time parameters in which to make a claim.

State laws regarding the disinheritance of a spouse are generally divided into four distinct categories.

First are the states that follow Uniform Probate Code guidelines as set forth in the early 1990s. These states tie the elective share percentage of a decedent's *augmented* estate to the number of years that the spouse was married to the decedent.

Second are states that disregard the number of years that the spouse and decedent were married and merely state a spouse's elective percentage in the estate, which may be the probate assets only or an augmented estate.

Third are states that have no elective share statute, but allow a surviving spouse to renounce a will and receive the intestate amount that the spouse would have received had the decedent not had a will.

Fourth are states that do not recognize a spouse's right to take an elective share. In those states, if it can be shown that the decedent intended to disinherit the spouse, the spouse may end up with nothing.

Mistrusted In-Laws

Perhaps you want your daughter to benefit from your estate—and your grandchildren to benefit someday, as well—but you do not want your son-in-law to control a penny of it. With proper planning, gifted or inherited property can be segregated from a beneficiary's marital assets. Not only can you keep the money out of the son-in-law's hands while he's married to your daughter; he shouldn't be able to touch it during a divorce. Make sure you talk to your daughter or leave a note for her emphasizing the need for her to scrupulously segregate her gifted and inherited assets from her marital assets if this is a concern.

No-Contest Provision

If your will or trusts have the potential to make one or more people very unhappy (perhaps you're giving unequal treatment to heirs), consider adding a section to the document disinheriting anyone who challenges your will or trust. This will not work on anyone you've disinherited completely; they have nothing to lose.

As a result, it sometimes makes sense to give an heir you would like to disinherit enough of a stake that she'll have to think twice before challenging your wishes. A truly devious heir—or perhaps an heir with a good attorney—might find a way to attack the will or trust without triggering this clause, but just seeing the language in the document is often an effective deterrent to a challenge.

These are just a few of the many circumstances that can be accounted for in a trust. Using trusts can help enable you and your family to effectively manage not only expected circumstances, but also provide help and guidance for unforeseen situations when you're gone.

Action Plan Twelve: Make the Tough Decisions!

A nine-step strategy for making difficult choices:

1. Consider whether all of your heirs can be trusted to act responsibly with their inheritances. Decide how much control they should have: Should someone else hold the purse strings? Should your heirs have access only for certain purposes? Should they have access to only a little bit at a time?

2. If you have any heirs who would be better off never inheriting directly, such as disabled family members whose government assistance is contingent on a low level of assets, consider a supplemental special-needs trust.

3. If there are family members you wish to partly or entirely disinherit, think about your reasons and spell them out to your lawyer when you meet.

Action Plan Twelve: Make the Tough Decisions!

4. If you want to attach conditions to certain gifts, discuss what you'd like to include in a values trust when you speak with your lawyer.

5. If you are married but have children from a previous marriage, consider how you'd like to divide your assets between your spouse and your children. Speak with your attorney about setting up a Q-TIP marital trust, if appropriate.

6. Make note of any additional trust provisions or other tools from this chapter that could be of use to you.

7. Determine whether your estate is large enough that estate taxes are a major threat. Usually, the threshold is in the $1 million neighborhood.

8. Consider how much inconvenience you're willing to put up with to reduce those estate taxes. Are you willing to:
- do some extra paperwork?
- do vast amounts of paperwork?
- pay large legal and accounting fees?
- give up some (or all) control of assets to your heirs prior to your death?
- rent your own home from your heirs?

If you're willing to go to these lengths, discuss your options for estate-tax reductions with your lawyer.

9. Act as soon as possible, especially if you're retired or nearing typical retirement age. Many of these techniques require considerable advance planning in order to be effective.

CHAPTER 13

Maintaining Your Estate Plan

"Spending my children's inheritance"
—Bumper sticker on luxury car

Once your estate plan is complete, just a few details remain. With the project so close to the finish line, it's important not to let these things slide—a mistake here can undo a lot of your hard work. Here are some answers to questions that always seem to come up at this stage of the process.

Where Should I Keep My Estate-Plan Documents?

Some attorneys keep all original documents and give clients photocopies or "conformed copies." Other attorneys give their clients all original documents and keep only photocopies in their files. If your attorney wants to keep the originals, ask about the safety of the location where they'll be kept.

Remember: Just because this attorney drafted and even holds the documents in safekeeping doesn't mean your family is obliged to hire her if legal assistance becomes necessary in carrying out the estate plan.

If the original documents are in your possession, it's vital that they be stored in a place safe from fire and theft, yet accessible when you die or if you become incapacitated. That usually means either a bank safe-deposit box or a fireproof safe in your home.

If the originals are kept at the bank in a safe-deposit box, a photocopy should be kept at home so you don't have to run to the bank or call your lawyer when you need to check something. Also, if the safe-deposit box is in your name, the bank might have to seal it upon your death.

It's often better to have joint access to the box with a spouse or other trusted person. The other joint-access holder should have a key to the box or at least know where the key is. Some states seal the box upon an owner's death even if there is a surviving signer, so be careful when using bank safe-deposit boxes to store your estate plans.

If you use a home safe for your documents, make sure someone you trust has the combination or an extra key. Security experts recommend bolting smaller safes to the frame of the house to prevent burglars from just taking the whole thing with them.

Details of insurance policies should also be accessible. Beneficiaries uncertain if they've missed any insurance policies can write to:

The American Council of Life Insurance
www.acli.com
Policy Search Department
1001 Pennsylvania Avenue, NW
Washington, DC 20004

Ask for a policy search form. When completed and returned, the form will be forwarded to member insurance companies who search their records and may provide the information necessary for an executor to file a claim on behalf of the estate.

FUNERAL FUN?

Why leave all the planning to others? Marty, known for his casual nature, specified that he be buried in cutoffs, T-shirt, and sandals and that blues music be played at his funeral. Amber directed there be no funeral or wake, but instead that there be a memorial service to celebrate her life. There were plenty of good stories, along with food and drink, to go around. Her trust specified that out-of-towners be reimbursed from the trust estate for their travel expenses.

Even if you don't want to think about these types of creative details, a note or memo stating your basic funeral and burial or cremation wishes should be kept with your will and trust documents. Alternatively, your instructions can be written into your will and/or power of attorney for health care.

Should I Discuss My Estate Plan with My Children?

There is little consensus on this point among the experts. It's a matter of your personal family dynamics and comfort level in discussing subjects such as money and death with your children. These can be especially delicate matters when you've decided to make unequal distributions in your estate plan.

On the one hand, if everyone, including the beneficiary who receives less than his siblings, knows of your intent, it can make it more difficult later on for the one who receives the short end of the stick to contest. On the other hand, some would say that it makes no sense to cause problems earlier than necessary. It's up to you.

Should I Consult with My Fiduciaries?

It's usually best to advise your fiduciaries—that is, your trustees, executors, guardians, and agents for property and health care—ahead of the time when they will be needed to act on your behalf.

It is also advisable to explain to your fiduciaries the circumstances under which they might have to act. If someone does not want to or cannot act, it's better to know at an early stage.

Some people may be concerned about hurt feelings in regards to the selection of trustee, executor, guardian, and agents. There is no doubt that making these choices is difficult and can cause bad feelings or jealousies. Do not let the fear of hurt feelings prevent you from doing your estate planning or lead you to select individuals who would otherwise not be your first, or even your second, choice.

HOW TO DEFEAT PROCRASTINATION

Use positive reinforcement to help you maintain your motivation and keep working on your estate plan.

Frequently tell yourself or write these phrases on paper and post them where you will see them often:

My family deserves my focused attention!
Providing for my family helps me sleep better at night!

How Often Should My Estate Plan Be Reviewed?

You must review your estate plan periodically to account for changing needs and life events. Here are some changes to be alert to because they should trigger a mandatory review with your attorney:

Have your children grown up since you did your will? _____

Are they now capable of making decisions on their own? _____

Can they now be trusted with large sums of money? _____

When a child reaches a point where you'd be comfortable leaving him money, your plan must be reviewed.

Have there been deaths, marriages, births, or divorces in your family? _____

Have you divorced, remarried, or had children since the last review? _____

In some states, a divorce will nullify a spousal bequest unless the bequest is renewed.

The documents I write generally provide for children born in the future, but certainly new children should make you think about these issues.

Are there family members who have special needs now? _____

If an heir is no longer able to care for himself, or make financial decisions on his own, the plan must be reviewed (see excerpted language from supplemental special-needs trust on pages 186–188).

Have any of your fiduciaries died, become disabled, moved, or otherwise changed to such a degree they might no longer be able to serve their intended function in your estate plan? _____

If so, your plan must be reviewed.

Is the size of your estate substantially different than it was when the plan was constructed or last reviewed? _____

Check the value of your:	Value at time of plan	Current
retirement plans		
stocks or other major investment accounts		
real estate		
any businesses owned		
death benefit of insurance policies		
any art, antiques, or collectibles of substantial value		
stock options		

If your net worth has increased substantially, you certainly should review your estate plan. Your circumstances might have changed since you and your lawyer last took a look at it, and laws might have changed as well.

Go through the above checklist periodically, perhaps once a year, to see if there is any particular reason to update your plan right away.

Most plans do not *require* an annual review with your lawyer, but certainly it makes sense to review the plan with him at least every three to five years. Even if nothing changes in your life (other than getting older), the law continually changes. If your lawyer retires, or you lose confidence in him, find a new attorney to do the review. Again, many attorneys will give you a free initial consultation, and either for free or for a small fee take a look at your current plan and give you comments on how he would update the plan.

Clients often ask me if it's okay to update their own plans, or do they need to see their lawyer for even the smallest alteration.

Certain changes can be made on one's own, including:

- Address changes. If one of your fiduciaries or beneficiaries moves from an address listed in a document, you can probably write the new address into the plan yourself without problem. But your attorney should be advised so she can update her records, and in any event she may feel more comfortable making those types of changes in a more formal manner.
- Specific personal property distributions, if handled properly in the first place. I recommend putting a reference in a will or trust to a separate list of assets drawn up by the client. So if you acquire new assets (the "stuff" mentioned earlier) or change who they're going to, it's a simple matter to make those changes yourself. Note, however, that this informal method is not as ironclad as listing items in the will or trust itself.
- New children or grandchildren—maybe. If an estate plan is written to account for the possibility of new additions to the family, there might be no need to head to your lawyer every time there's a birth. Discuss this with your lawyer when the plan is drawn up.

From a commonsense perspective, many other changes *do* require the attention of an attorney. Crossing off or writing in the names of new heirs or changing the percentages that people receive is not something that you want to be in the habit of doing, because such informal changes may not withstand attack from someone who feels slighted.

When you meet with your lawyer to review your estate plan, the structure of your estate—how assets are owned and various beneficiary designations—should be reviewed along with your documents.

What Needs to Be Done Regarding Social Security?

When you die, your beneficiaries should contact the Social Security Administration (800-772-1213).

Monthly benefits might be available for certain beneficiaries, including:

- a surviving spouse
- minor children
- divorced spouses
- parents who were financially dependent on the decedent

In addition, your estate might be eligible to receive a onetime death benefit of $255—supposedly for burial. If you're not certain that your beneficiaries will remember to call the Social Security Administration, leave a note with your estate plan explaining what to do.

What Will Happen to My Estate If I Require a Long Stay in a Nursing Home?

One of the most gut-wrenching situations that occurs in estate planning involves families depleting their hard-earned assets to pay for nursing-home care.

Medicare may pay for a maximum one hundred days in a nursing home. After that, people must pay (and pay and pay) until they have depleted substantially all their assets. With the average cost of a one-year stay in a nursing home exceeding $40,000, nursing home care can quickly drain a nest egg that it took a lifetime to build.

Another government program, Medicaid, a component of the federal welfare system, will pay for long-term care under certain circumstances—but only when the patient has little if any money left.

Under current law, to qualify for Medicaid your assets and those of your spouse have to be minimal—no more than about $90,000 in most states. Unfortunately, some people find that divorcing their longtime spouses is the only answer to preserving their estate.

Certain assets, such as a principal residence, might be exempt, but this varies from state to state. In the past, some people have sought to protect their assets and simultaneously qualify for Medicaid by using complex trusts and divestment strategies to conceal assets. But recent federal and state laws have made this very difficult, and lawyers who help clients pursue this strategy can find themselves in trouble.

Often, people seek to "spend down" their assets to qualify for Medicaid by transferring assets to their children. But when the government determines your Medicaid eligibility it typically will include transfers made to other individuals over the past three years or so as continuing to be part of your estate, as well as transfers made to trusts over the past five years or so, although these rules vary from state to state.

Thus, those seeking to qualify for Medicaid without giving up the bulk of their assets must plan long in advance and find a way to support themselves for perhaps three to five years or more with few remaining assets.

WHO IS THE CLIENT?

A type of meeting many estate-planning lawyers dread is with adult children who want advice on qualifying their parents for Medicaid. Besides the fact that various government agencies have tried to put an end to this strategy, there is another problem facing the attorney, namely, Who is the client, the parent or the child?

Usually, the client is the person whose assets are being spent down, and without her cooperation, efforts in this area can cause problems for all concerned. A lawyer could in good faith help adult children transfer Mom's assets to her descendants, thinking this is what she would want if she were in her right mind, then wind up in court with Mom saying, "They stole my money," and pointing out the attorney "who helped them."

Another option for protecting an estate from the costs of nursing homes is long-term-care insurance, or nursing-home insurance. This insurance can pay for either a nursing home or for in-home health care. Like any other insurance, cost of coverage depends on age, health, deductibles, and various limitations.

While it is growing in popularity, long-term-care coverage can be expensive and makes most sense for those who have substantial estates to protect, but not enough to handle long-term-care bills out-of-pocket without feeling the pinch—say those with anywhere from $200,000 to $1 million in net worth.

Will My Estate Plan Be Effective If I Move to Another State?

Estate-planning law is fairly uniform throughout the United States, but there are still many differences among states. In an attempt to unify the various state laws, many states have enacted a statute known as the Uniform Probate Code. This code has been adopted by most, but not all, states.

The U.S. Constitution requires that "full faith and credit shall be given in each state to the public acts, records and judicial proceedings of every other state." This means, generally speaking, that a legal document is valid anywhere in the country if it is valid in the state in which it was signed. So if you have signed a will, trust, or power of attorney that is valid in the state in which it is signed it should be valid nationwide, and even in other countries.

However, if you move to another state after doing an estate plan, it is prudent to review your documents with an attorney in the new state. This is particularly true if you move to or from a community property (CP) state. Community property states classify marital assets as belonging equally between the spouses, and the planning and asset structures differ sharply between CP and non-CP states.

As of 2002, community property states included Arizona, California, Idaho, Louisiana, Nevada, New Mexico, Texas, Washington, and Wisconsin.

No attorney understands the legal nuances of every state. If you move to another state and intend to become a permanent resident, have your estate plan reviewed by an attorney located there who concentrates a significant portion of his or her practice on estate planning.

What Record Keeping Needs to Be Done with Purchases I Make?

Record keeping can be tedious, but it might be a money saver should the IRS challenge a tax return. Many investors fail to keep track of their assets' cost basis, which is the price they paid for major purchases. When you inherit assets, ask the executor of the estate for the value of the asset at the time of the owner's death and record it. That value is your basis.

If you have failed to keep records, there are ways to find out your basis. For example, if you inherited shares of a publicly traded corporation, your stockbroker can find the value of the stock on the date of death of the person who bequeathed the shares to you.

If you were gifted stock, determining its basis is more difficult and time-consuming because you must determine its value at the time it was first purchased. If the stockbroker can't help you, try the corporation whose stock it is, or the transfer agent, listed on the share certificate. With their help, it might be possible to determine the stock's basis as of the date of the gift, although a stock purchased thirty years ago may have split ten times and had its name changed or been acquired just as many times. Compound that with shares acquired at various times through a dividend-reinvestment plan and you have lots of homework to do. It can definitely get confusing!

If the asset is real estate, a real estate agent or appraiser with access to historical data should be able to prepare something for you that is acceptable to the IRS.

For what it's worth, the step-up in basis is scheduled to be eliminated at the same time that the estate tax is scheduled to be eliminated, but again, the Sunset provision scheduled to take place after December 31, 2010, may change that as well.

Is There Any Other Major Money Planning I Need to Do?

Estate planning does not replace financial planning. A financial plan is a determination of your present and future financial needs and goals, and a strategy for getting you there.

Financial planners can provide asset-allocation models and make specific investment recommendations in accordance with an overall strategy to accomplish various goals. While financial planning clearly is intertwined with estate planning, I believe you'll be better off asking a financial planner, rather than an estate-planning attorney, for assistance in such objectives as preserving principal or providing a certain income stream.

A financial planner who is not an attorney is prohibited from drafting estate-plan documents. If you use both a financial planner and an estate-planning attorney, these professionals should work together to give you a comprehensive plan that works for you and your family.

REAL-LIFE STORIES

Gerald, 72, and Martha, 70, had not bothered to review their estate plan in the ten years prior to their death. They didn't think it was necessary: There had been no additions to their family, or subtractions from it. The size of their estate had not altered significantly, and they had made no major purchases.

But it turned out that a review would have been wise. While their situation had not changed, that of one of their key fiduciaries had: Martha's brother Carl had died. He had seemed the rational choice for the role of trustee, since he had been a successful money manager for decades. The couple's backup trustee, Carl, Jr., also was a money manager, but had shown nowhere near his father's skill since taking over his father's business seven years earlier. If it had occurred to them, Gerald and Martha would have picked a different trustee.

Don't Delay!

As soon as your estate plan is complete, supply a list of your important documents and their locations to your family and your legal and financial advisers. These likely include:

- a will (regular will or pour-over will)
- a living trust
- a durable power of attorney for property
- a durable power of attorney for health care
- any insurance policies

- a list of assets, particularly those that your heirs might have trouble tracking down, as discussed in chapter 4
- any other important financial documents

Action Plan Thirteen: Celebrate!

A four-step strategy to keep everything in place:

1. Find a secure place to keep your estate-plan documents.

2. Share the details of this location with family members and make sure they have access to it in an emergency.

3. Discuss the basics of the plan with your fiduciaries, at least as the plan relates to them. Make changes to your fiduciary designations if there is reason to believe that the people you have selected will not be able to serve adequately.

4. Plan to review the documents *at least* every three to five years. It's easy to forget things that occur so rarely, so it might help to tie your reviews to some major event that recurs on this cycle, perhaps the Olympics, presidential elections or years ending with a five or a zero—whatever you feel you'll be able to remember.

Estate planning might not be anyone's idea of fun, but handled properly, and with the assistance of a competent lawyer familiar with estate planning and the issues unique to your family, you've probably found that it need not become an overwhelming burden, either.

Congratulations on completing your estate plan! All that remains is keeping the plan up-to-date. If you've come this far, it would be a shame to see those efforts wasted. If you've yet to sit down with an estate planning attorney, now is the time. Remember, it's up to you: Either handle your own estate planning now, or let the government and courts do it for you the difficult and expensive way.

GLOSSARY

"I like to pay my taxes. With them I buy civilization."
—Oliver Wendell Holmes

Accounting—A detailed analysis of income, gains, losses, transactions, and assets that may be required of a trustee or executor. A trust and will may require accounting for certain situations or waive the need for it in other situations.

Administration—The management and settlement of an estate in probate court. Similar in usage to the term "probate."

Administrator (fem.: administratrix)—The person appointed by the probate court to handle an administration when there is no will or where the executor or executors named in the will are unable to serve.

Agent—Under a power of attorney, the person granted the legal right to act on behalf of the principal. Also sometimes referred to as an attorney-in-fact.

Alternate valuation date—In an estate-tax return, IRS Form 706, the executor can choose to value the estate by its fair market value on the decedent's date of death, or on the alternate valuation date, precisely six months after the date of death. If the assets have declined in value, this may be a useful tool to cut estate taxes.

Ancillary jurisdiction—A jurisdiction outside the state where the decedent officially resided. If a decedent owns real estate in more than one state, his estate may be subject to probate in each state in which the real estate is located. By retitling real estate owned outside the state of residence into a trust, multiple ancillary probates may be avoided.

Annual exclusion amount—Each person may gift up to $11,000 per year to any other person without incurring any gift tax. Gifts in excess of $11,000 will result in a partial or full use of the maximum applicable exclusion amount and require a gift-tax filing. There is no limit on the number of $11,000 gifts you can make to different people in a year. To qualify for this exclusion, the gift must be of a present interest, meaning that the recipient can enjoy the gift immediately. Annual exclusion gifts are often used creatively to deplete estates with prospective estate-tax problems.

Applicable exclusion amount—The amount that you can leave to your designated heirs (other than your spouse, in most cases) without incurring any estate or gift tax.

Ascertainable standards—Language describing, and in some cases limiting, how trust income and principal can be used by a trustee for a beneficiary. A common example is, "The trustee can use the trust's income for the beneficiary's health, maintenance in reasonable comfort, and education."

Basis—The acquisition cost of an asset, used to calculate gains and losses.

Beneficiary—A person who receives or benefits from a will, trust, or contractual property such as insurance, qualified plans, annuities, or transferable-(payable-)-on-death accounts.

Bequest—Assets transferred to a beneficiary under a will.

Bond—A guarantee by an insurance company or bonding agency to repay any loss due to negligence or criminal cause by an executor, administrator, or trustee. A will or revocable living trust can waive any bond requirement.

Buy-sell agreement—A contractual agreement among partners or shareholders of a business that specifies the terms for buying out one partner's or shareholder's share upon his retirement, death, or disability.

Capital gain—The profit reported to the IRS upon the sale of a capital asset. Capital gain is the difference between the basis cost of an asset and the net proceeds of the sale of the asset. If the asset is sold for a lower price than its acquisition cost, a capital loss may be reported.

Charitable remainder trust—The donation of an asset to a charity in which the donor reserves the right to use the property or receive income from it for a specified period of time, perhaps years or even lifetimes. When the agreed period is over, the property belongs to the charity.

Codicil—A document that amends or supplements a will. It must be executed with the same degree of formality as a will.

Community property (CP)—Community-property states (currently Arizona, California, Idaho, Louisiana, Nevada, New Mexico, Texas, Washington, and Wisconsin) provide that a husband and wife each own a one-half interest in the other's assets and earnings during the course of the marriage. States that are not community-property states provide for separate property rights during the course of the marriage. In most community-property states, the only separate property is that which is owned exclusively by one of the spouses prior to the marriage and never commingled with community property and assets received by gift or inherited at any time.

Conservator—A type of guardian appointed by a probate court to manage the affairs of a mentally incapacitated adult.

Contingent fiduciary—The backup to the successor trustee, executor, guardian, or agent, should that person be unable or unwilling to act.

Credit shelter trust—A trust designed to protect the unified credit that each person may gift or bequeath to heirs. This is often referred to as a bypass trust because the trust assets more or less bypass the surviving spouse and are not included in her estate. Still, the surviving spouse can have certain rights in the trust during her lifetime. It also is referred to as the "B" trust in an "A-B" trust. Since the unified credit has been replaced by the applicable exemption amount under the Tax Relief Act of 2001, the term "credit shelter trust" is now more accurately referred to as the "applicable exemption amount shelter trust"—same effect, new terminology.

Crummey power—The right of a donor to make gifts to a trust with a withdrawal right. The donor or trustee must notify the beneficiary of his Crummey rights to withdraw some or all of the value of the gift in the year made. The right to withdraw—which is typically not exercised—is required for the donation to the trust to be a gift of a present interest.

Custodian—The person or organization managing assets for minor children or adults deemed incompetent.

Death probate—The process of legally validating a will or intestate estate. It involves collecting assets, paying bills, and eventually retitling the assets, all under the supervision of the probate court. For living probate, see "Guardianship." All types of probate can be substantially avoided and its costs minimized though proper estate planning.

Decedent—A person who has died, whether testate or intestate (that is, with or without a will).

Descendant—A person who is a relative in a direct vertical line from another person—children, grandchildren, great-grandchildren, and so forth.

Disclaimer—A person inheriting assets can refuse to accept any or all of those assets. Disclaimers can be very useful in certain situations, especially if they have been anticipated and planned for. An effective disclaimer is governed by strict state and federal laws. Among other things, a disclaimer must be in writing and made within nine months of a person's death.

Domicile—The state or county where a person primarily resides, determining the taxing and probate jurisdictions.

Donee—A person who receives a gift or bequest or to whom a power of appointment is given.

Donor—See "Grantor."

Durable power of attorney for health care—Document allowing your agent to direct your health care if you are unable to do so, avoiding a guardianship of the person. As with the durable power of attorney for property, it is durable because, unlike an ordinary power of attorney, it survives a subsequent incompetence.

Durable power of attorney for property—A document in which you grant an agent the authority to handle financial matters should you become disabled. The document is used to avoid a financial guardianship proceeding in court, which is a type of living probate.

Escheat—The process by which assets of a person who dies intestate (without a will), without heirs, go to the state.

Estate tax—A transfer tax that the federal government and some states assess on the right to transfer assets to others on your death. Sometimes referred to as the death tax or, incorrectly, as inheritance tax.

Executor (fem.: executrix)—A person, bank, or trust company designated in your will to administer your estate upon your death, under the supervision of the probate court. More than one executor can act together as co-executors. Referred to in some states as a personal representative.

Family Limited Liability Company (FLLC)—(see Family Limited Partnership)

Family Limited Partnership (FLP)—A legal entity created by state statute that serves estate planning and asset protection needs.

Fiduciary—A person in a position of trust and responsibility, subject to heightened legal and ethical standards, including, among others, trustees, executors, guardians, and agents.

Generation-skipping transfer tax (GST tax)—An additional transfer tax assessed on gifts and bequests in excess of $1 million to grandchildren, great-grandchildren, or anyone at least two generations below the donor. Language allocating the $1 million exemption from the tax can be included in a generation-skipping trust as part of the overall trust or will.

Gift—A voluntary transfer of property to another made without receiving something of equal value. A completed gift, which removes an asset from a donor's estate, must be of a present interest and without any conditions. The federal government will assess a gift tax when the value of the gift exceeds the annual exclusion and the unified credit is exhausted.

Grantor—The person who establishes a trust and transfers his own assets to it. Also called the trustor, settler, or donor.

Grantor trust—A trust in which the grantor retains control of the assets or income. The income from a grantor trust is taxable to the grantor rather than to the beneficiary, although the grantor and beneficiary may be one and the same.

Guardian—The person appointed by a probate court, often designated in your will, to be responsible for your children or an incompetent adult. In the case of the incompetent adult, also known as a conservator.

Guardianship—The probate court process of administration or management of the property or person of minor children and incompetent adults, a type of living probate. Guardianships of incompetent adults can generally be avoided though the use of trusts and durable powers of attorney if signed while the person is still competent.

Heirs—The persons who receive your assets under a will or following your death if you die intestate.

Incidents of ownership—Any element of control or ownership rights in an insurance policy. To remove insurance from a gross estate for estate-tax purposes, you must give up all incidents of ownership and live at least three years.

Incompetence—The inability of a person to function and take care of his or her own affairs, sometimes referred to as a legal disability or incapacity.

Inheritance tax—A tax levied by some states on the right of heirs to inherit assets. An inheritance tax is imposed on the heir rather than on the estate.

Intentionally defective grantor trusts (IDGTs)—Income-tax-shifting trusts in which a grantor irrevocably transfers assets, usually by partial gift and partial sale, out of his estate but still pays the income taxes on earnings and capital gains, even though paid to the beneficiaries.

Inter vivos trust—See "Revocable living trust."

Intestate—Dying without a valid will. When a person dies intestate, the probate court—following state intestacy laws—will determine who is to receive assets, act as administrator, and act as guardian for minor children.

Inventory—A list of all assets contained in a probate estate. A probate estate inventory is a matter of public record, available for examination by anyone who cares to ask for it.

Irrevocable trust—A trust that cannot be amended or revoked by its grantor(s). Like corporations, these are separate tax entities. Irrevocable trusts are often used in estate planning to place assets outside of someone's estate. One of the most common types of irrevocable trust is the irrevocable life-insurance trust (ILIT), which is intended primarily to prevent insurance death benefits from being included in your taxable estate.

Joint tenancy with right of survivorship (JTWROS)—Shared ownership between two or more people, with the survivor(s) owning the property after the death of one or more fellow joint tenants. This delays probate, but ultimately does not avoid it. Moreover, it may result in income- and estate-tax pitfalls along with unintended liabilities. Compare with "Tenancy in common."

Legacy—Property transferred by your will. The person receiving a legacy is the legatee.

Letters testamentary—Term used in some jurisdictions to refer to the legal document that provides the proper authority for an executor to act for the estate of a deceased person. Also referred to as "letters of office."

Living trust—See "Revocable trust."

Living will—A statement of philosophy concerning your desire for treatment in the case of extreme injury or illness, if the procedures in question are only going to delay the dying process. The living will is generally considered a less important health care directive than the health care power of attorney.

No-contest clause—A clause in some wills and trusts that purports to disinherit any person attempting to attack the validity of such will or trust. Does this work? Sometimes, depending on the court and the equities involved. If the beneficiary has something substantial to lose, it may at least give him pause before contesting the document.

Payable-on-death account (POD)—A type of bank or brokerage account that avoids probate. If a person has a very limited net worth and very limited beneficiaries with no complicating factors, this may be a useful tool. Also referred to as a transfer-on-death account (TOD).

Per capita—A distribution made equally to a number of persons without regard to generation. A distribution to "all my descendants equally and per capita" would result in children, grandchildren, and great-grandchildren each receiving the same amount. This is generally a less prevalent distribution pattern than per stirpes distributions.

Per stirpes—Latin for "by the branch," the method of dividing assets among descendants so that such descendants as a class take the share that the ancestor would have been entitled to take had the ancestor survived.

Pour-over will—A will used in conjunction with a revocable living trust stating that all remaining assets are to be transferred ("poured over") to the trust. Even where there is a fully funded trust, you should have a pour-over will.

Power of appointment—The right to transfer or dispose of property that you do not own, such as assets in a trust created by someone else. If estate-tax planning is involved, care must be taken that the power is not a general power, in which case the assets subject to the power may unintentionally be included in the estate of the person who has the power. A special power limits the authority of the person holding the power to transfer assets, perhaps restricting transfers to a particular class of persons, such as to the descendants of the original donor, to charities, or for ascertainable standards. In a general-power-of-appointment marital trust (as opposed to a Q-TIP marital trust), the surviving spouse can withdraw as much of the principal trust as she desires whenever she desires.

Precatory language—Suggestive language in a will or trust that expresses your sentiments or preferences, but is not binding.

Principal—(1) The assets that make up a trust, sometimes referred to as the corpus. Many trusts provide for separate treatment of principal and income derived from the principal. (2) The person who confers authority on an agent in a power of attorney.

Probate—See "Death Probate."

Probate court—A state court where probate estates are administered. In some jurisdictions, a magistrate's court or surrogate court handles probate functions.

Qualified domestic trust (QDOT)—Special language that must be part of the marital trust portion of a revocable living trust if the surviving spouse is not a U.S. citizen.

Qualified S corporation trust (QSST)—A trust that contains special provisions to enable a trust to own S corporation stock.

Qualified terminable interest in property trust (Q-TIP)—A type of marital trust that qualifies for the unlimited marital exclusion, but does not give the surviving spouse a general power of appointment. Q-TIPs limit the rights of the surviving spouse in such a way that the assets are preserved for a different beneficiary at the surviving spouse's subsequent death. As with any marital trust, the surviving spouse must receive all of the trust's income during his or her lifetime and can, under certain circumstances, also receive portions of principal. This can be especially useful where there is a second marriage and the grantor wishes to protect the children from the first marriage while benefiting the surviving spouse during his or her lifetime.

Remainder—The assets remaining in an estate for a beneficiary or heir, after an income or other temporary interest has ended.

Residuary—The assets remaining in an estate after all specific transfers of property are made and all expenses are paid. When a pour-over will is used, the residuary is transferred to a trust.

Retitling—(1) The process that legally transfers ownership of property from the grantor to the revocable living trust. Without retitling assets, a revocable living trust is unfunded and will not work efficiently as a means to avoid probate. (2) The portion of the probate process that, at the court's direction, transfers ownership of assets from the decedent to the heirs or beneficiaries.

Revocable living trust—A trust established by the grantor during his lifetime. A revocable living trust can be amended (changed), or revoked (canceled) at any time during the grantor's lifetime. Sometimes called an inter vivos (Latin for "while living") trust, also interchangeable with "revocable trust" and "living trust."

Rule against perpetuities—A common-law principle that prevents a person from reaching out from the grave to control his assets forever. A trust interest must vest not more than "twenty-one years plus a life in being." (Check out the movie *Body Heat*, in which William

Hurt's character is tripped up by the rule.) In recent years, some states have, by statute, enacted laws enabling people to set up their estates so as to opt out of the rule.

S corporation—A corporation whose income is taxed to its shareholders, thus avoiding a corporate tax. Only certain trusts may own S corporation shares.

Section 2503(c) trust—An irrevocable trust established for minor children. Gifts to such trusts are deemed to be gifts of a present interest and thus can qualify for the annual $11,000 gift-tax exclusion. The trustee manages the trust assets and, at her discretion, may distribute income or principal to a beneficiary until the beneficiary reaches age twenty-one. At that point, the beneficiary has the right either to withdraw the trust assets or to leave the trust intact until a later date. This type of trust is generally more flexible than a Uniform Transfers to Minors Act (UTMA) account and is a good choice for removing assets from a grantor's estate in favor of a minor.

Self-declaration of trust—A type of revocable living trust in which the grantor is also the trustee and therefore controls the assets of the trust.

Settler—See "Grantor."

Spendthrift provision—A clause in a trust that prevents a beneficiary from spending an inheritance without restraint and also may prevent creditors from reaching the beneficiary's interest in the trust.

Sprinkle power—A trustee's right to distribute income in any proportion to several named beneficiaries. Such a power gives the trustee the discretion to distribute money according to the relative needs of the beneficiaries.

Stepped-up basis—The rule that makes an heir's cost basis equal to the value of the asset at the date of the grantor's death—or, alternatively, six months later—rather than its original cost. If a gift of an appreciated asset is made during the donor's lifetime, the donee takes the donor's original cost basis and there is no step-up in the basis. The step-up avoids a capital-gains tax on the appreciation that occurred during the donor's lifetime. The step-up rule is scheduled to end in 2010, but could be brought back the following year by the Sunset provision of the Tax Relief Act of 2001.

Successor trustee—Under a self-declaration of trust, the backup to the grantor, who is the initial trustee. The document can provide for successors to act individually or collectively. The same holds true for other fiduciaries.

Sunset provision—A provision in a law that ends the law at a certain date as if the law never existed. The Tax Relief Act of 2001 contains a Sunset provision that activates after the year 2010, eliminating the repeal of estate taxes.

Survivorship insurance—A life-insurance policy that insures a couple instead of an individual. It can be much less expensive than an individual insurance policy. Its purpose is usually to pay the estate taxes that arise after the death of the surviving spouse and is most useful where the decedent's assets are predominantly illiquid, such as real estate or a family corporation. In order to be properly utilized, the policy should be held outside the insureds' estate, possibly in an irrevocable insurance trust. Also commonly referred to as a second-to-die policy.

Tangible personal property—Movable property such as jewelry, clothing, automobiles, etc., as opposed to real property (land and buildings) or intangibles such as stocks, bonds, and bank accounts.

Tenancy by the entirety—A special type of joint tenancy available in some states for a husband and wife who own their principal residence, it protects the residence from creditors and liability claims against one of the spouses. As with a regular joint tenancy, this delays but does not eliminate probate.

Tenancy in common—An undivided interest in property. Unlike a joint tenancy interest, there is no right of survivorship to the remaining tenants in common. Different types of entities may be tenants in common. If the tenant in common who dies is an individual, there may be a need to probate. Property also may be owned by more than one trust as tenants in common.

Testamentary trust—A trust created under a will and activated upon death. In and of itself, it does not necessarily avoid probate.

Testator (fem.: testatrix)—A person who creates and executes a valid will.

Trust—A legal written arrangement in which one or more trustees hold and manage assets for the benefit of one or more beneficiaries under a fiduciary relationship.

Trustee—The person or company acting in a fiduciary capacity managing and administering trust assets for the benefit of one or more beneficiaries.

Trustor—See "Grantor."

Unified credit—A tax credit applied to gift or estate taxes. The Tax Relief Act of 2001 changed the terminology to "applicable exclusion amount," and it is not unified anymore, because inheritances and gifts are treated differently after 2003.

Uniform Transfers to Minors Act (UTMA)—A method of holding property for the benefit of a minor. It is simple to set up, but less flexible than a 2503(c) trust or Crummey trust.

Unlimited marital deduction—A rule permitting spouses to transfer an unlimited amount of assets to each other, while alive or after death, without any income- or estate-tax implications. Overuse of the unlimited marital deduction may lead to a loss of the unified credit of the first spouse to die.

Will—A legal document completed in accordance with state law that lays out how your assets will be distributed on your death. The will appoints an executor to administer your estate and may establish trusts for children and recommend guardians for minor children.

Will contest—A legal challenge to a will, usually made by one or more disgruntled heirs, which can result in great expense to the estate and tie up the estate for great lengths of time. Will contests often are based on allegations that the will was improperly executed or that the decedent lacked proper mental capacity at the time he created the will or that someone exerted undue influence on the decedent.

State Survey 1—Intestacy—Laws of Descent and Distribution

The laws of intestacy apply when you die with no will or trust, and if there are no surviving designated beneficiaries or joint tenants. Except where otherwise stated, all distributions are of the net estate—after all expenses are paid and homestead deductions and other exemptions subtracted.

Most distributions summarized below are per stirpes. For instance, when referring to children, if there is a deceased child or other relation, then any share that that child or other relation would have received had he or she survived will usually be distributed to that person's descendants, if any. For instance, if a share is distributed to brothers and sisters equally and per stirpes, then any deceased brother or sister's share will go to that deceased person's descendants, your nieces and nephews (and great-nieces and -nephews if there are deceased nieces or nephews).

If there is no surviving spouse, descendants, parents, siblings, nephews, or nieces, then the following information will not help you. Even though the laws of descent and distribution of the various states do extend farther than what is presented below, they are too detailed and confusing for the purposes of this book. In *most* cases, in the absence of a spouse, descendant, parent, sibling, nephew, or niece, an intestate estate will then transfer to maternal and paternal grandparents or great-grandparents and their descendants, who are uncles, aunts, great-uncles and -aunts, and cousins of various degrees.

In a few states, some of which are noted, if there is no surviving family whatsoever, the families of deceased spouses may be entitled to an intestate share. Also, in most though not all states, half brothers and half sisters are treated the same as full siblings, and that may also extend to other "half" relatives.

If you have never been married and have no family descending from your grandparents or even great-grandparents, your estate will likely escheat—meaning it is transferred to the state in which you live, with real estate going to the county in which it is located.

Do not rely on the following information in lieu of doing a proper estate plan. Many nuances of the various states are not fully explained here, and some of the laws, in fact, may be different from those detailed below.

Alabama

Surviving spouse and children who are all both decedent's and spouse's: $50,000 plus half of balance to spouse and half of balance to children, equally and per stirpes.

Surviving spouse and children, including children not of spouse: Half to spouse and half to children, equally and per stirpes.

Surviving spouse, but no children: $100,000 plus half of balance to spouse and half of balance to parents in equal shares, or, if only one parent is living, to the surviving parent or, if no parent, all to spouse.

No spouse or children surviving: All to parents in equal shares or, if only one parent is living, all to the surviving parent, or, if no parent, then to brothers and sisters, equally and per stirpes.

Alaska

Surviving spouse and children who are all both decedent's and spouse's: $50,000 plus half of balance to spouse and balance to children, equally and per stirpes.

Surviving spouse and children, including children not of spouse: Half to spouse and half to children, equally and per stirpes.

Surviving spouse, but no children: $50,000 plus half of balance to spouse and half of balance to parents in equal shares or, if only one parent is living, to the surviving parent, or, if no parent, all to spouse.

No spouse or children surviving: All to parents in equal shares or, if only one parent is living, all to the surviving parent, or, if no parent, then to brothers and sisters, equally and per stirpes.

Arizona—Community Property

Surviving spouse and children who are all both decedent's and spouse's: All of decedent's separate property plus half of decedent's community property to spouse and half of decedent's community property to children equally and per stirpes.

Surviving spouse and children, including children not of spouse: Half of decedent's separate property to spouse and half of decedent's separate property plus all of decedent's community property to children, equally and per stirpes.

Surviving spouse, but no children: All to spouse.

Surviving children, but no spouse: All to children equally and per stirpes.

No spouse or children surviving: All to parents in equal shares or, if only one parent is living, all to the surviving parent, or, if no parent, then to brothers and sisters, equally and per stirpes.

Arkansas

Surviving spouse and children who are all both decedent's and spouse's: Real estate: one-third life estate to spouse and balance to children, equally and per stirpes. Personal property: one-third to spouse and two-thirds to children, equally and per stirpes.

Surviving spouse and children, including children not of spouse: Real estate: one-third life estate to spouse and balance to children, equally and per stirpes; Personal property: one-third to spouse and two-thirds to children, equally and per stirpes.

Surviving spouse, but no children: All to spouse if married over three years. If married less than three years, half to spouse and half to parents in equal shares or, if only one parent is living, to the surviving parent, or, if no parent, to brothers and sisters, per stirpes; or, if none, then to ancestors up to great-grandparents' generation and descending, per stirpes; or, if none, all to spouse.

Surviving children, but no spouse: All to children equally or to their children, per capita.

No spouse or children surviving: All to parents in equal shares or, if only one parent is living, all to the surviving parent, or, if no parent, then to brothers and sisters, equally and per stirpes.

Arkansas statutes state that if all members of the class who inherit real or personal property from an intestate are related to the intestate in equal degree, they will inherit the intestate's estate in equal shares and will be said to take per capita. If the inheritors are of unequal degree, then those in the nearer degree will take per capita or in their own right; those in the more remote degree will take per stirpes.

California—Community Property

Surviving spouse: All community property and quasi-community property passes to the spouse.

Surviving spouse and child(ren): Half of separate property to spouse and half to one child (or to that child's descendants, per stirpes, if the child is deceased) if there is only one child. If there is more than one child, one-third goes to the spouse and two-thirds to the children, equally and per stirpes.

Surviving spouse, but no children: Half of separate property to the spouse and half to the parents in equal shares or, if only one parent is living, to the surviving parent, or, if no parent, to brothers and sisters, equally and per stirpes or, if none, all to spouse.

Surviving children, but no spouse: All to children, equally and per stirpes.

No spouse or children surviving: All to parents in equal shares or, if only one parent is living, all to the surviving parent, or, if no parent, then to brothers and sisters, equally and per stirpes.

There is a special provision in California that if a single person dies without a living spouse, children, or grandchildren, and had previously inherited from a predeceased spouse, that which was previously inherited from that spouse goes back to the predeceased spouse's nearest relatives. These provisions apply only when there is real estate involved and the two spouses die within fifteen years of each other, or when there is personal property (all assets other than real property), and both spouses die within a five-year period.

The California statutes specifically allow foster children and stepchildren to inherit intestate estates from foster parents and stepparents in certain instances.

Colorado

Surviving spouse and children who are all both decedent's and spouse's only: All to spouse.

Surviving spouse and children, including children not of spouse: Half to spouse and half to children, equally and per stirpes.

Surviving spouse and children, but spouse, besides having children with decedent, also has children who are not decedent's: Spouse receives the first $150,000, plus half of balance and balance to children, equally and per stirpes.

Surviving spouse and any children who are not children of spouse's: (1) If all surviving children are adults, spouse receives the first $100,000, plus half of balance and balance to children, equally and per stirpes; or (2) If any surviving children are minors, then half only to spouse and balance to children, equally and per stirpes.

Surviving spouse, but no children of either decedent or spouse: First $200,000 plus three-fourths of balance to spouse and balance to parents in equal shares or, if only one parent is living, to the surviving parent, or, if none, all to spouse.

Surviving children, but no spouse: All to children, equally and per stirpes.

No spouse or children surviving: All to parents in equal shares or, if only one parent is living, all to the surviving parent, or, if no parent, then to brothers and sisters, equally and per stirpes.

The Colorado laws of intestacy, rather than mentioning a per stirpes distribution, instead state that distributions are "per capita at each generation." I am sure that there must be a difference, but I do not know what it is.

Connecticut

Surviving spouse and children who are all both decedent's and spouse's: $100,000 plus half of balance to spouse and balance to children, equally and per stirpes.

Surviving spouse and children, including children not of spouse: Half to spouse and half to children, equally and per stirpes.

Surviving spouse, but no children: $100,000 plus three-quarters of balance to spouse and balance to parents in equal shares or, if only one parent is living, to the surviving parent, or, if no parent, all to spouse.

Surviving children, but no spouse: All to children, equally and per stirpes.

No spouse or children surviving: All to parents in equal shares or, if only one parent is living, all to the surviving parent, or, if no parent, then to brothers and sisters, equally and per stirpes.

Delaware

Surviving spouse and children who are all both decedent's and spouse's: Real estate: Life estate to spouse and balance to children, per stirpes; Personal property: $50,000 plus half of balance to spouse and balance to children, equally and per stirpes.

Surviving spouse and children not of spouse: Real estate: Life estate to spouse and balance to children, equally and per stirpes; Personal property: half to spouse and half to children, equally and per stirpes.

Surviving spouse, but no children: Real estate: Life estate to spouse and balance to parents in equal shares or, if only one parent is living, to the surviving parent, or, if neither parent is living, to the parents' then living descendants, collectively and per stirpes. Personal property: $50,000 plus half of balance to spouse and balance to parents in equal shares or, if only one parent is living, to the surviving parent, or, if no parent, all to spouse.

Surviving children, but no spouse: All to children, equally and per stirpes.

No spouse or children surviving: All to parents in equal shares or, if only one parent is living, all to the surviving parent, or, if no parent, then to brothers and sisters, equally and per stirpes.

District of Columbia

Surviving spouse and children: Real estate: one-third life estate to spouse and balance to children, per stirpes; Personal property: one-third to spouse and two-thirds to children, equally and per stirpes.

Surviving spouse, but no children: Real estate: one-third life estate to spouse and balance to parents in equal shares or, if only one parent is living, to the surviving parent, or, if no parent, then to brothers and sisters, equally and per stirpes, or, if none, to more remote kin, unless there are neither grandparents nor grandparents' descendants, in which case all to spouse. Personal property: half to spouse and half to parents in equal shares or, if only one parent is living, to the surviving parent, or, if no parent, then to brothers and sisters, equally and per stirpes, or, if none, to more remote kin, unless there are neither grandparents nor grandparents' descendants, in which case all to spouse.

Surviving children, but no spouse: All to children, equally and per stirpes.

No spouse or children surviving: All to parents in equal shares or, if only one parent is living, all to the surviving parent, or, if no parent, then to brothers and sisters, equally and per stirpes.

Florida

Surviving spouse and children who are all both decedent's and spouse's: $20,000 plus half of balance to spouse and balance to children, equally and per stirpes.

Surviving spouse and children not of spouse: Half to spouse and half to children, equally and per stirpes.

Surviving spouse, but no children: All to spouse.

Surviving children, but no spouse: All to children, equally and per stirpes.

No spouse or children surviving: All to parents in equal shares or, if only one parent is living, all to the surviving parent, or, if no parent, then to brothers and sisters, equally and per stirpes.

Georgia

Surviving spouse and children: Spouse and children (equally and per stirpes) all get equal shares, with at least one-quarter going to spouse.

Surviving spouse, but no children: All to spouse.

Surviving children, but no spouse: All to children equally and per stirpes.

No spouse or children surviving: All to surviving parents, brothers, and sisters, equally and per stirpes.

Hawaii

Surviving spouse and children: Half to spouse and half to children, equally and per stirpes.

Surviving spouse, but no children: Half to spouse and half to parents in equal shares or, if only one parent is living, to the surviving parent, or, if no parent, all to spouse.

Surviving children, but no spouse: All to children, equally and per stirpes.

No spouse or children surviving: All to parents in equal shares or, if only one parent is living, all to the surviving parent, or, if no parent, then to brothers and sisters, equally and per stirpes.

Idaho—Community Property

Surviving spouse and children who are all both decedent's and spouse's: All of decedent's community property to spouse; $50,000 plus half of balance of decedent's separate property to spouse and balance to children, equally and per stirpes.

Surviving spouse and children not of spouse: All of decedent's community property to spouse; half of decedent's separate property to spouse and half to children, equally and per stirpes.

Surviving spouse, but no children: All of decedent's community property to spouse; $50,000 plus half of balance of decedent's separate property to spouse and balance to parents in equal shares or, if only one parent is living, to the surviving parent, or, if no parent, all to spouse.

Surviving children, but no spouse: All to children, equally and per stirpes.

No spouse or children surviving: All to parents in equal shares or, if only one parent is living, all to the surviving parent, or, if no parent, then to brothers and sisters, equally and per stirpes.

Illinois

Surviving spouse and children: Half to spouse and half to children, equally and per stirpes.

Surviving spouse, but no children: All to spouse.

Surviving children, but no spouse: All to children, equally and per stirpes.

No spouse or children surviving: All to parents, brothers, and sisters (and the descendants, collectively and per stirpes, of any deceased brother or sister) in equal parts, allowing to the surviving parent if one is deceased a double portion. If no brothers or sisters or their descendants, all to parents in equal shares or, if only one parent is living, all to the surviving parent. If no parent, then all to brothers and sisters, equally and per stirpes.

Indiana

Surviving spouse and children who are all both decedent's and spouse's: Half to spouse and half to children, equally and per stirpes.

Surviving spouse and children not of spouse: Real estate: Life estate in real estate to spouse and balance to children, equally and per stirpes; Personal property: third to spouse and two-thirds to children, equally and per stirpes (unless there is only one child, in which case half to spouse and half to child).

Surviving spouse, but no children: Three-quarters to spouse and one-quarter to parents in equal shares or, if only one parent is living, to the surviving parent, or, if no parent, all to spouse.

Surviving children, but no spouse: All to children, equally and per stirpes.

No spouse or children surviving: All to parents, brothers, and sisters (and the descendants, collectively and per stirpes, of any deceased brother or sister); parents receive at least half if both are living, and one-quarter if only one parent is living. If no brothers or sisters or their descendants, all to parents in equal shares or, if only one parent is living, all to the surviving parent. If no parent, then all to brothers and sisters, equally and per stirpes.

Iowa

Surviving spouse and children who are all both decedent's and spouse's: All to spouse.

Surviving spouse and children not of spouse: $50,000 plus half of balance to spouse and balance to children, equally and per stirpes.

Surviving spouse, but no children: All to spouse.

Surviving children, but no spouse: All to children, equally and per stirpes.

No spouse or children surviving: All to parents in equal shares or, if only one parent is living, all to the surviving parent, or, if no parent, then to brothers and sisters, equally and per stirpes.

Iowa, in calculating the intestate division of personal property, distinguishes between that which is exempt from execution and that which is not.

Kansas

Surviving spouse and children: Half to spouse and half to children, equally and per stirpes.

Surviving spouse, but no children: All to spouse.

Surviving children, but no spouse: All to children, equally and per stirpes.

No spouse or children surviving: All to parents in equal shares or, if only one parent is living, all to the surviving parent, or, if no parent, then to brothers and sisters, equally and per stirpes.

Kentucky

Surviving spouse and children: Real estate: Life estate of third of property acquired during marriage plus half of other real estate to spouse and balance to children, equally and per stirpes. Personal property: half to spouse and half to children, equally and per stirpes.

Surviving spouse, but no children: Half to spouse and half to parents in equal shares or, if only one parent is living, to the surviving parent, or, if no parent, then the balance to brothers and sisters, equally and per stirpes, or, if none, all to spouse.

Surviving children, but no spouse: All to children, equally and per stirpes.

No spouse or children surviving: All to parents in equal shares or, if only one parent is living, all to the surviving parent, or, if no parent, then to brothers and sisters, equally and per stirpes.

Louisiana—Community Property

Louisiana is the only state that uses Napoleonic code, based upon French laws predating the Louisiana purchase, rather than common law, which is based upon (originally) British case law.

Surviving spouse and children: All community property to children, equally and per stirpes, except spouse has the right to use the property until remarried. All separate property to children, equally and per stirpes.

Surviving spouse, but no children: All community property to spouse. All separate property to brothers and sisters, equally and per stirpes, or, if none, to parents in equal shares, or, if only one parent is living, to the surviving parent, or, if none of the above, all to spouse.

Surviving children, but no spouse: All to children, equally and per stirpes.

No spouse or children surviving: All to brothers and sisters, equally and per stirpes, or, if none, to parents in equal shares, or, if only one parent is living, all to the surviving parent.

Maine

Surviving spouse and children who are all both decedent's and spouse's: $50,000 plus half of balance to spouse and balance to children, equally and per stirpes.

Surviving spouse and children not of spouse: Half to spouse and half to children, equally and per stirpes.

Surviving spouse, but no children: $50,000 plus half of balance to spouse and balance to parents in equal shares, or, if only one parent is living, to the surviving parent, or, if none, to the parents' children, per capita, or, if none, to more remote kin.

Surviving children, but no spouse: All to children, equally and per stirpes.

No spouse or children surviving: All to parents in equal shares, or, if only one parent is living, all to the surviving parent, or, if no parent, then to brothers and sisters, equally and per capita.

Maryland

Surviving spouse and children: If any surviving children are minors, half to spouse and half to children, equally and per stirpes. If no surviving children are minors, $15,000 plus half of balance to spouse and balance to children, equally and per stirpes.

Surviving spouse, but no children: $15,000 plus half balance to spouse and balance to parents in equal shares, or, if only one parent is living, to the surviving parent, or, if no parent, all to spouse.

Surviving children, but no spouse: All to children, equally and per stirpes.

No spouse or children surviving: All to parents in equal shares, or, if only one parent is living, all to the surviving parent, or, if no parent, then to brothers and sisters, equally and per stirpes.

Massachusetts

Surviving spouse and children: Half to spouse and half to children, equally and per stirpes.

Surviving spouse, but no children: $200,000 plus half of balance to spouse and balance to parents in equal shares, or, if only one parent is living, to the surviving parent, or, if no parent, to brothers and sisters, equally and per stirpes, or, if none, to next of kin, or, if none, all to spouse.

Surviving children, but no spouse: All to children, equally and per stirpes.

No spouse or children surviving: All to parents in equal shares, or, if only one parent is living, all to the surviving parent, or, if no parent, then to brothers and sisters, equally and per stirpes.

Michigan

Surviving spouse and children who are all both decedent's and spouse's: $60,000 plus half of balance to spouse and balance to children, equally and per stirpes.

Surviving spouse and children not of spouse: Half to spouse and half to children, equally and per stirpes.

Surviving spouse, but no children: $60,000 plus half of balance to spouse and balance to parents in equal shares, or, if only one parent is living, all to the surviving parent, or, if no parent, then all to spouse.

Surviving children, but no spouse: All to children, equally and per stirpes.

No spouse or children surviving: All to parents in equal shares, or, if only one parent is living, all to the surviving parent, or, if no parent, then to brothers and sisters, equally and per stirpes.

Minnesota

Surviving spouse and children who are all both decedent's and spouse's: $70,000 plus half of balance to spouse and balance to children, equally and per stirpes.

Surviving spouse and children not of spouse: Half to spouse and half to children, equally and per stirpes.

Surviving spouse, but no children: Half to spouse and half to parents in equal shares, or, if only one parent is living, all to the surviving parent, or, if no parent, then all to spouse.

Surviving children, but no spouse: All to children, equally and per stirpes.

No spouse or children surviving: All to parents in equal shares, or, if only one parent is living, all to the surviving parent, or, if no parent, then to brothers and sisters, equally and per stirpes.

Mississippi

Surviving spouse and children: Spouse and any surviving children take equal shares, with deceased children's shares descending per stirpes.
Surviving spouse, but no children: All to spouse.
Surviving children, but no spouse: All to children, equally and per stirpes.
No spouse or children surviving: All to parents, brothers, and sisters equally, with deceased brother's and sister's shares descending per stirpes. If no brothers or sisters or their descendants, all to parents in equal shares, or, if only one parent is living, all to the surviving parent. If no parent, then all to brothers and sisters, equally and per stirpes.

Missouri

Surviving spouse and children all both decedent's and spouse's: $20,000 plus half of balance to spouse and balance to children, equally and per stirpes.
Surviving spouse and children not of spouse: Half to spouse and half to children, equally and per stirpes.
Surviving spouse, but no children: All to spouse.
Surviving children, but no spouse: All to children, equally and per stirpes.
No spouse or children surviving: All to parents, brothers, and sisters equally, with deceased brother's and sister's shares descending per stirpes. If no brothers or sisters or their descendants, all to parents in equal shares, or, if only one parent is living, all to the surviving parent. If no parent, then all to brothers and sisters, equally and per stirpes.

Montana

Surviving spouse and children all both decedent's and spouse's: All to spouse.

Surviving spouse and children not of spouse: If one child, half to spouse and half to child (or descendants of deceased child, per stirpes); if more than one child surviving, third to spouse and two-thirds to children, equally and per stirpes.

Surviving spouse, but no children: All to spouse.

Surviving children, but no spouse: All to children, equally and per stirpes.

No spouse or children surviving: All to parents in equal shares, or, if only one parent is living, all to the surviving parent, or, if no parent, then to brothers and sisters, equally and per stirpes.

Nebraska

Surviving spouse and children all both decedent's and spouse's: $50,000 plus half of balance to spouse and balance to children, equally and per stirpes.

Surviving spouse and children not of spouse: Half to spouse and half to children, equally and per stirpes.

Surviving spouse, but no children or parents: All to spouse.

Surviving spouse, but no children: $50,000 plus half of balance to spouse and balance to parents in equal shares, or, if only one parent is living, to the surviving parent, or, if no parent, all to spouse.

Surviving children, but no spouse: All to children, equally and per stirpes.

No spouse or children surviving: All to parents in equal shares, or, if only one parent is living, all to the surviving parent, or, if no parent, then to brothers and sisters, equally and per stirpes.

Nevada—Community Property

Surviving spouse and children: All of decedent's community property to spouse. If only one child (or descendants of deceased child), half of decedent's separate property to spouse and half to child; if more than one child, one-third of separate property to spouse and two-thirds to the children, equally and per stirpes.

Surviving spouse, but no children: All of decedent's community property to spouse. Half of decedent's separate property to spouse and half to parents in equal shares, or, if only one parent is living, to the surviving parent, or, if no parent, to brothers and sisters, equally and per stirpes, or, if none of the above, all to spouse.

Surviving children, but no spouse: All to children, equally and per stirpes.

No spouse or children surviving: All to parents in equal shares, or, if only one parent is living, all to the surviving parent, or, if no parent, then to brothers and sisters, equally and per stirpes.

New Hampshire

Surviving spouse and children all both decedent's and spouse's: $50,000 plus half of balance to spouse and balance to children, equally and per stirpes.

Surviving spouse and children not of spouse: Half to spouse and half to children, equally and per stirpes.

Surviving spouse, but no children: $50,000 plus half of balance to spouse and balance to parents in equal shares, or, if only one parent is living, to the surviving parent, or, if no parent, all to spouse.

Surviving children, but no spouse: All to children, equally and per stirpes.

No spouse or children surviving: All to parents in equal shares, or, if only one parent is living, all to the surviving parent, or, if no parent, then to brothers and sisters, equally and per stirpes.

New Jersey

Surviving spouse and children who are all both decedent's and spouse's: $50,000 plus half of balance to spouse and balance to children, equally and per stirpes.

Surviving spouse and children not of spouse: Half to spouse and half to children, equally and per stirpes.

Surviving spouse, but no children: $50,000 plus half of balance to spouse and balance to parents in equal shares, or, if only one parent is living, to the surviving parent, or, if no parent, all to spouse.

Surviving children, but no spouse: All to children, equally and per stirpes.

No spouse or children surviving: All to parents in equal shares, or, if only one parent is living, all to the surviving parent, or, if no parent, then to brothers and sisters, equally and per stirpes.

New Mexico—Community Property

Surviving spouse and children: All of decedent's community property to spouse. One-quarter of decedent's separate property to spouse and three-quarters to children, equally and per stirpes.

Surviving spouse, but no children: All to spouse.

Surviving children, but no spouse: All to children, equally and per stirpes.

No spouse or children surviving: All to parents in equal shares, or, if only one parent is living, all to the surviving parent, or, if no parent, then to brothers and sisters, equally and per stirpes.

New York

Surviving spouse and children: $50,000 plus half of balance to spouse and balance to children, equally and per stirpes.

Surviving spouse, but no children: $25,000 plus half of balance to spouse and balance to parents in equal shares, or, if only one parent is living, to the surviving parent or, if none, all to spouse.

Surviving children, but no spouse: All to children, equally and per stirpes.

No spouse or children surviving: All to parents in equal shares, or, if only one parent is living, all to the surviving parent, or, if no parent, then to brothers and sisters, equally and per stirpes.

North Carolina

Surviving spouse and children: If only one child (or descendants of deceased child), $15,000 (only from personal property, if any) plus half of balance to spouse and balance to child. If more than one-child, $15,000 (only from personal property, if any) plus one-third of balance to spouse and balance to children, equally and per stirpes.

Surviving spouse, but no children or parents: All to spouse.

Surviving spouse and parent(s), but no children: $25,000 (from personal property, if any) plus half of balance to spouse and balance to parents in equal shares, or, if only one parent is living, all to the surviving parent.

Surviving children, but no spouse: All to children, equally and per stirpes.

No spouse or children surviving: All to parents in equal shares, or, if only one parent is living, all to the surviving parent, or, if no parent, then to brothers and sisters, equally and per stirpes.

North Dakota

Surviving spouse and children who are all both decedent's and spouse's: $50,000 plus half of balance to spouse and balance to children equally and per stirpes.

Surviving spouse and children not of spouse: half to spouse and half to children, equally and per stirpes.

Surviving spouse, but no children: $50,000 plus half of balance to spouse and balance to parents in equal shares, or, if only one parent is living, to the surviving parent, or, if no parent, all to spouse.

Surviving children, but no spouse: All to children, equally and per stirpes.

No spouse or children surviving: All to parents in equal shares, or, if only one parent is living, all to the surviving parent, or, if no parent, then to brothers and sisters, equally and per stirpes.

Ohio

Surviving spouse and children who are all both decedent's and spouse's: All to spouse.

Surviving spouse and one child who is not of spouse: $20,000 plus half of balance to spouse and balance to child (or descendants of deceased child, equally and per stirpes).

Surviving spouse and more than one child not of spouse: $60,000 if the spouse is the natural or adoptive parent of one, but not all, of the children, or the first $20,000 if the spouse is the natural or adoptive parent of none of the children, plus one-third of the balance to spouse and the balance to the children, equally and per stirpes.

Surviving spouse, but no children: All to spouse.

Surviving children, but no spouse: All to children, equally and per stirpes.

No spouse or children surviving: All to parents in equal shares, or, if only one parent is living, all to the surviving parent, or, if no parent, then to brothers and sisters, equally and per stirpes.

Oklahoma

Surviving spouse and children all both decedent's and spouse's: half to spouse and half to children, equally and per stirpes.

Surviving spouse and children not of spouse: (1) an undivided half interest in the property acquired by the joint industry of the husband and wife during the marriage, and (2) an undivided equal part in the property of the decedent not acquired by the joint industry of the husband and wife during the marriage to the spouse and balance to children, equally and per stirpes.

Surviving spouse, but no children: All property acquired by the joint industry of the husband and wife during the marriage plus one-third of other property to spouse and balance to parents in equal shares, or, if only one parent is living, to the surviving parent, or, if no parent, to brothers and sisters, equally and per stirpes, or, if none of the above, all to spouse.

Surviving children, but no spouse: All to children, equally and per stirpes.

No spouse or children surviving: All to parents in equal shares, or, if only one parent is living, all to the surviving parent, or, if no parent, then to brothers and sisters, equally and per stirpes.

Oregon

Surviving spouse and children all both decedent's and spouse's: All to spouse.

Surviving spouse and children not of spouse: half to spouse and half to children, equally and per stirpes.

Surviving spouse, but no children: All to spouse.

Surviving children, but no spouse: All to children, equally and per stirpes.

No spouse or children surviving: All to parents in equal shares, or, if only one parent is living, all to the surviving parent, or, if no parent, then to brothers and sisters, equally and per stirpes.

Pennsylvania

Surviving spouse and children who are all both decedent's and spouse's: $30,000 plus half of balance to spouse and balance to children, equally and per stirpes.

Surviving spouse and children not of spouse: half to spouse and half to children, equally and per stirpes.

Surviving spouse, but no children: $30,000 plus half of balance to spouse and balance to parents in equal shares, or, if only one parent is living, to the surviving parent, or, if no parent, all to spouse.

Surviving children, but no spouse: All to children, equally and per stirpes.

No spouse or children surviving: All to parents in equal shares, or, if only one parent is living, all to the surviving parent, or, if no parent, then to brothers and sisters, equally and per stirpes.

Rhode Island

Surviving spouse and children: Real estate: Life estate to spouse and balance to children, equally and per stirpes. Personal property: half to spouse and half to children, equally and per stirpes.

Surviving spouse, but no children: Real estate: Life estate plus $75,000 to spouse (upon court approval), balance to parents in equal shares, or, if only one parent is living, to the surviving parent, or, if no parent, to brothers and sisters, equally and per stirpes, or, if none, half to maternal and half to paternal grandparents, or, if none, to aunts and uncles equally or their children, per stirpes, or, if none, to the next of kin, or, if none of the above, all to the spouse. Personal property: $50,000 plus half of balance to spouse and balance same as for real estate.

Surviving children, but no spouse: All to children, collectively and per stirpes.

No spouse or children surviving: All to parents in equal shares, or, if only one parent is living, all to the surviving parent, or, if no parent, all to brothers and sisters, equally and per stirpes.

South Carolina

Surviving spouse and children: half to spouse and half to children, equally and per stirpes.

Surviving spouse, but no children: All to spouse.

Surviving children, but no spouse: All to children, collectively and per stirpes.

No spouse or children surviving: All to parents in equal shares, or, if only one parent is living, all to the surviving parent, or, if no parent, then to brothers and sisters, equally and per stirpes.

South Dakota

Surviving spouse and children: If only one child, half to spouse and half to child (or descendants of deceased child, equally and per stirpes). If more than one child, one-third to spouse and two-thirds to children, equally and per stirpes.

Surviving spouse, but no children: $100,000 plus one half of balance to spouse and balance to parents in equal shares, or, if only one parent is living, to the surviving parent, or, if no parent, to brothers and sisters, equally and per stirpes, or, if none of the above, all to spouse.

Surviving children, but no spouse: All to children, equally and per stirpes.

No spouse or children surviving: All to parents in equal shares, or, if only one parent is living, all to the surviving parent, or, if no parent, all to brothers and sisters, equally and per stirpes.

Tennessee

Surviving spouse and children: Family homestead plus one year's support allowance plus child's share (at least one-third) to spouse and balance to children, equally and per stirpes.

Surviving spouse, but no children: All to spouse.

Surviving children, but no spouse: All to children, equally and per stirpes.

No spouse or children surviving: All to parents in equal shares, or, if only one parent is living, all to the surviving parent, or, if no parent, all to brothers and sisters, equally and per stirpes.

Texas—Community Property

Surviving spouse and children who are all both decedent's and spouse's: Community estate: All to spouse. Separate property: Separate real property goes one-third life estate to spouse and balance to children, equally and per stirpes. Separate personal property goes one-third to spouse and two-thirds to children, equally and per stirpes.

Surviving spouse and children not of spouse: Community property: half to spouse and half to children, equally and per stirpes. Separate property: one-third of personal estate and life estate and one-third of real estate to spouse and balance to children, equally and per stirpes.

Surviving spouse and no children: All of personal estate to spouse plus half of real estate and balance to parents in equal shares, or, if only one parent is living, to the surviving parent, or, if no parent, to brothers and sisters, equally and per stirpes, or, if none, to grandparents and their descendants, per stirpes, or, if none of the above, all to spouse.

Surviving children, but no spouse: All to children, equally and per stirpes.

No spouse or children surviving: All to parents in equal shares, or, if only one parent is living, all to the surviving parent, or, if no parent, all to brothers and sisters, equally and per stirpes.

Utah

Surviving spouse and children who are all both decedent's and spouse's: All to spouse.

Surviving spouse and children not of spouse: $50,000 to spouse, plus half of balance, and balance to children, equally and per capita at each generation.

Surviving spouse, but no children: All to spouse.

Surviving children, but no spouse: All to children, equally and per capita at each generation.

No spouse or children surviving: All to parents in equal shares, or, if only one parent is living, all to the surviving parent, or, if none, all to parents' descendants, equally and per capita at each generation.

As far as I can tell, "per capita at each generation" has the same effect as "per stirpes," but I could be wrong.

Vermont

Surviving spouse and children all both decedent's and spouse's: Personal property: up to one-third (judicially determined) plus all household goods and wearing apparel and balance to children, equally and per stirpes. Real estate: If only one child, half to spouse and half to child (or descendants of deceased child, equally and per stirpes). If more than one child, one-third to spouse and two-thirds to children, equally and per stirpes.

Surviving spouse, but no children: If no spousal election is made, $25,000 plus half to spouse and balance to parents in equal shares, or, if only one parent is living, to the surviving parent, or, if no parent, to brothers and sisters, equally and per stirpes, and so on.

Surviving children, but no spouse: All to children, equally and per stirpes.

No spouse or children surviving: All to parents in equal shares, or, if only one parent is living, all to the surviving parent, or, if no parent, all to brothers and sisters, equally and per stirpes.

Note that Vermont allows for same-sex "civil unions" whereby the surviving partner of the civil union has the same intestate rights as a surviving spouse.

Virginia

Surviving spouse and children all both decedent's and spouse's: All to spouse.

Surviving spouse and children not of spouse: One-third to spouse and two-thirds to children, equally and per stirpes.

Surviving children, but no spouse: All to children, equally and per stirpes.

No spouse or children surviving: All to parents in equal shares, or, if only one parent is living, all to the surviving parent, or, if no parent, then to brothers and sisters, equally and per stirpes.

Washington—Community Property

Surviving spouse and children: All of decedent's community property plus half of decedent's separate property to spouse and balance to children, equally and per stirpes.

Surviving spouse, but no children: All of decedent's community property plus three-quarters of decedent's separate property to spouse and balance to parents in equal shares, or, if only one parent is living, to the surviving parent, or, if no parent, to brothers and sisters, equally and per stirpes, or, if none of the above, all to spouse.

Surviving children, but no spouse: All to children, equally and per stirpes.

No spouse or children surviving: All to parents in equal shares, or, if only one parent is living, all to the surviving parent, or, if no parent, all to brothers and sisters, equally and per stirpes.

West Virginia

Surviving spouse and children all both decedent's and spouse only: All to spouse, provided that no other descendant of the surviving spouse survives the decedent.

Surviving spouse and children, but spouse, besides having children with decedent, also has children who are not decedent's: If all of the decedent's surviving children are also children of the spouse and the spouse has one or more surviving descendants who are not descendants of the decedent, three-fifths to spouse and two-fifths to children, equally and per stirpes.

Surviving spouse and children not of spouse: half to spouse and half to children, equally and per stirpes (presuming spouse has no other children).

Surviving spouse, but no children: All to spouse.

Surviving children, but no spouse: All to children, equally and per stirpes.

No spouse or children surviving: All to parents in equal shares, or, if only one parent is living, all to the surviving parent, or, if no parent, then to brothers and sisters, equally and per stirpes.

Wisconsin—Community Property

Surviving spouse and children all both decedent's and spouse's: All to spouse.

Surviving spouse and children not of spouse: half to spouse and half to children, equally and per stirpes.

Surviving spouse, but no children: All to spouse.

Surviving children, but no spouse: All to children, equally and per stirpes.

No spouse or children surviving: All to parents in equal shares, or, if only one parent is living, all to the surviving parent, or, if no parent, then to brothers and sisters, equally and per stirpes.

Wyoming

Surviving spouse and children: Half to spouse and half to children, equally and per stirpes.

Surviving spouse, but no children: All to spouse.

Surviving children, but no spouse: All to children, equally and per stirpes.

No spouse or children surviving: All to parents, brothers, and sisters equally, with deceased brother's and sister's shares descending per stirpes. If no brothers or sisters or their descendants, all to parents in equal shares, or, if only one parent is living, all to the surviving parent. If no parent, then all to brothers and sisters, equally and per stirpes.

State Survey 2. Use of Small Estate Affidavits in Lieu of Probate

Please note that trust assets, assets that are owned jointly with a surviving joint tenant, and assets that designate a surviving beneficiary (such as insurance policies and payable-on-death accounts) are not subject to probate and as such are not subject to the considerations that govern whether an estate can avoid probate through the use of an affidavit.

Also note that, except where otherwise stated, real estate cannot be transferred by the affidavit process.

If there is individually owned real estate, it must nearly always be probated in the county and state in which it is located. Unless otherwise stated, the values listed below are net equity values after liens and encumbrances are subtracted.

View this table as a general rule of thumb rather than a definitive rule, because there are various twists within the individual states and the laws can and do change. As indicated by the "N/A" designation, not all states provide for the use of affidavits to short-circuit a probate.

State	Small Estate Affidavits and the Maximum Values for which They Can Be Used
Alabama	N/A
Alaska	Maximum estate—$15,000.
Arizona	Maximum estate—$30,000 (or, if the claimant is a surviving spouse or dependent child, less than the greater of either $30,000 or the family allowances allowed by law, the amount of which depends on the circumstances).
Arkansas	N/A
California	Maximum estate—$100,000, excluding any manufactured or mobile home, vessel, or motor vehicle; salary up to $5,000; and amounts due decedent for services in the armed forces. For real estate valued up to $20,000, claimants can file a simple affidavit with the probate court and then record a certified copy with the county recorder.
Colorado	Maximum estate—$27,000.
Connecticut	N/A
Delaware	Maximum estate—$20,000. Available only to spouse, certain other relatives, and funeral director.
District of Columbia	Maximum estate—Only for one or two motor vehicles.
Florida	N/A
Georgia	N/A
Hawaii	Maximum estate—$20,000 value of Hawaiian assets.
Idaho	Maximum estate—$25,000.
Illinois	Maximum estate—$50,000.
Indiana	Maximum estate—$15,000.
Iowa	Maximum estate—$10,000 gross value.
Kansas	Maximum estate—$10,000.
Kentucky	N/A

State	Small Estate Affidavits and the Maximum Values for which They Can Be Used
Louisiana	Maximum estate—$50,000
Maine	Maximum estate—$10,000.
Maryland	N/A
Massachusetts	N/A
Michigan	N/A
Minnesota	Maximum estate—$20,000.
Mississippi	N/A
Missouri	N/A
Montana	Maximum estate—$7,500.
Nebraska	Maximum estate—$25,000.
Nevada	Maximum estate—$10,000 gross value of Nevada assets (and no Nevada real estate). Available only to surviving spouse, children, grandchildren, parents, or siblings.
New Hampshire	N/A
New Jersey	N/A
New Mexico	1. Surviving spouse may use affidavit to gain title to community property principal residence if valued at less than $100,000 for property tax purposes and if no other assets require probate. 2. Maximum estate for other property—$30,000.
New York	N/A
North Carolina	N/A
North Dakota	Maximum estate—$15,000.
Ohio	N/A
Oklahoma	N/A

State	Small Estate Affidavits and the Maximum Values for which They Can Be Used
Oregon	N/A
Pennsylvania	N/A
Rhode Island	Maximum estate—$10,000, not counting tangible personal property. Available only to surviving spouse, next of kin, or person who paid funeral bill. Funeral bill must be paid first.
South Carolina	Maximum estate—$10,000 or less. Affidavit must be approved by probate judge.
South Dakota	Maximum estate—$15,000.
Tennessee	N/A
Texas	Maximum estate—$50,000, not including homestead and exempt property. Affidavit must be approved by probate judge. Can be used to transfer homestead, but no other real estate.
Utah	Maximum estate—$25,000 or less.
Vermont	N/A
Virginia	Maximum estate—$10,000.
Washington	Maximum estate—$60,000, not counting surviving spouse's community property interest.
West Virginia	N/A
Wisconsin	Maximum estate—$10,000 value of Wisconsin assets.
Wyoming	Maximum estate—$70,000.

Photo by Arielle R. Matlin

Eric G. Matlin received his law degree from the John Marshall Law School in Chicago in 1978. He is the founding partner in the law firm of Matlin & Fajerstein in Northbrook, Illinois, and an original founding director of the Greater North Shore Estate and Financial Planning Council, which provides continuing education to lawyers, estate planners, and CPAs. He has worked with thousands of families on their estate plans. His clients range from people with a negative net worth to people with more than $10 million. He lives with his wife and children in Glencoe, Illinois. For more information, visit his Web site at www.ericmatlin.com.